Diary of a Man in Despair

Friedrich Percyval Reck-Malleczewen

*Translated by Paul Rubens
with an Introduction by
Norman Stone*

Duck Editions

Second impression March 2000
Complete translation first published in February 2000 by
Duckworth Literary Entertainments, Ltd.
61 Frith Street, London W1V 5TA
Tel: 0207 434 4242
Fax: 0207 434 4420
email: DuckEd@duckworth-publishers.co.uk
www.ducknet.co.uk

Original version published in Germany in 1947 by Burger Verlag
under the title *Tagebuch eines Verzweifelten*.

German Language Copyright © Henry Goverts Verlag GmbH, Stuttgart
1966

First American Edition published in 1979 by
The Macmillan Company
866 Third Avenue, New York, N.Y. 10022
Collier-Macmillan Canada Ltd., Toronto, Ontario

First British Edition published in 1995 by
Audiogrove Limited
102 Jermyn Street, London

A CIP catalogue record for this title is available from the British Library.

ISBN 0 7156 3000 8

: Doyle & Associates, Liverpool
d in Great Britain by
Books Ltd, Trowbridge

RO

ary c . . . . .. Despair

Introduction

Norman Stone

This remarkable book is hybrid: a highly educated North German, given to the cosmic pessimism that distinguished many of his Nietzschean vintage, the 1880s, keeping anti-Nazi diaries in Bavaria before and during the war. There is a common misapprehension that Bavaria was the most enthusiastically Nazi part of Germany: not so. The small *Meistersinger* towns of the *romantische Strasse* south of Würzburg, which were preserved by geography from the otherwise shattering Allied bombings of 1944–45, were indeed quite strongly Nazi, and were Protestant islands in a countryside that was a Catholic sea. But most of Bavaria voted for the Catholic party, not the Nazis.

Reck-Malleczewen, like other educated, upper-class North Germans, was deeply mistrustful of the modern world. The Nazis only confirmed his cynicism. But, living in Bavaria, his encounters are with Catholicism – not formally so, of course, but these diaries are an interesting literary testimony to something that, in Germany today, matters. For, in the Federal Republic, the wreckage of one Germany, largely Protestant and Prussian, was subsumed in another, dominated by Catholics from the south and west. This underlies what Reck-Malleczewen memorably confides to his diaries.

'Anti-fascism' became a watchword of the Left, and for many years after the Second World War, it was a useful device for Communists to seize power: any non-Communist, as in Central

Europe, could simply be called 'Fascist' and hauled off. It often happened that people who had been in Fascist jails went back into the same jails, now Communist, and guarded, often enough, by the same warders, who had turned coats.

This ignored an important element in modern German history: that anti-Fascists had quite often been men of the Right. The very word 'Nazi' stood for 'National Socialist', and men of the upper classes were often suspect. In the winter of 1944-45, when Reck-Malleczewen was arrested, for the second time, as we now learn with the inclusion of the recently discovered chapter, he was one among many. Indeed this moment is the most poignant part of the diary.

The future Federal Republic – peaceful, allied with the West, democratic, and sometimes stuffily law-bound – owed much to these non-Communist anti-Nazi elements. For them, Reck-Malleczewen speaks, and does so with powerful contempt. His diaries, translated (very well) in the United States some thirty years ago, are a fluent account of the disintegration of Germany in wartime by a highly intelligent conservative whose pessimism gave him qualities highly desirable in a writer – black humour, contempt and resilience. (Graham Greene says somewhere that every writer should have a sliver of ice in his heart, which often makes writers rather unattractive characters.)

Reck-Malleczewen seems at times almost to gloat at the bombing of Germany – retribution, laced with surreal humour. The French writer, Louis-Ferdinand Céline (*Nord* and *D'un château l'autre*), responded in the same way, on a vast scale. He had, however, taken his hatred for the modern world to the point of espousing the Nazi cause – he was Marshal Pétain's doctor, and spoke viciously on the radio as a propagandist – on the grounds that, if you wanted destruction of that mean, petty-bourgeois world, the people whom Reck-Malleczewen dismisses as *canaille*, you would get it more efficiently and profoundly through the Nazis than ever through the Communists. Céline is of course about as politically incorrect as it is possible to be, though the modern reader now, guiltily, maybe finds his great set-pieces of black surrealism (they have been translated into Russian) rather better to tuck up with than the old goody-goodies of the *Front Popu* era. Does anyone, nowadays, read, say, Gide without reflecting, 'hard cheese, old chap'?

Reck-Malleczewen is no Céline, of course. He would have been associated, had he survived the war, with that group of old-fashioned moralists known as the *Ordoliberalen*, high-minded Hayekians who had been solidly anti-Nazi before and during the war (and in some cases in exile) and who were the chief makers, after 1949, of the West German 'economic miracle'.

Reck-Malleczewen had an interesting background. One clue in the diaries – he does not much talk about it, otherwise – comes in a throw-away line, praising a certain 'Heydebrand' as conservative leader. This was a certain Ernst von Heydebrand und der Lasa, one of those resonantly Teutonic names that stud the lists of the German conservative party before 1914: Graf von Arnim-Boitzenburg, Freiherr von Oldenburg-Januschau, Graf von Kanitz-Podangen, Graf zu Reventlow, Graf Westarp – not big aristocrats at all, but a samurai, what Frederich the Great had called the *rocher de bronze* on which the Hohenzollern monarchy stood. A few had Polish names, Hutten-Czapski, Podbielski, for that matter Malleczewen, as a good part of Prussia had originally been Polish and Catholic, but in general these were arch-Prussians, whose dislikes were fairly comprehensive.

Ernst von Heydebrand und der Lasa comes across, in the modern history of the *Kaiserzeit*, as rather a bogey-man: reactionary to the end. Their fathers had even been hostile to Bismarck, on the grounds that Bismarck, by fusing Protestant Prussia in partly Catholic Germany, was ruining her character. Upon unification in 1871, Prussia, in fact, preserved a great part of her historic character. Bismarck allowed universal male suffrage for the Reichstag that was set up for united Germany. The Prussian conservatives did not like this one bit: what, the mob (Reck-Malleczewen's *canaille*) having the same voting-weight as their betters? *Unerhört! Unverschämt!* How could you possibly extend the voting to elements so un-Prussian: *Polaken! Katholen! Proletenjanhagel!* They even expelled Bismarck, one of their own, from the Junkers' league. But the Prussian parliament was not the Reichstag. It legislated for the two-thirds of Germany that was under Prussian control, and it did not like Catholics. There was only one Prussian Catholic minister in the entire Kaiserreich, and even he had married a Protestant, agreeing to bring up his children as such.

Franz von Papen, the man who did most, later on, to bring Hitler to power, was the only Prussian guards officer of Catholic background: he came from an old Catholic family in Westphalia, and had married into quite serious money (as it happens, the heiress of Villeroy and Bosch, the largest German manufacturer of lavatory pans). The Prussian conservatives were utterly determined not to extend the vote. They could not quite deprive the masses of it – this was, after all, the nineteenth century – but they could make sure that each vote did not count for the same. They instituted what was called the 'three-class franchise'. The top third of tax-payers voted in one electoral group, for a third of the electoral college *Wahlmänner* who would actually elect the deputies, and the next-top third for another, and so on. The result was that the masses were effectively disenfranchised – a handful of social democratic deputies, and far fewer Catholics than their numbers might have warranted. There was some compensation, in that the upper chamber, the *Herrenhaus*, contained men appointed because of their office: professors, no less, and lord mayors (Adenauer, much later on, remembered that house, of which, being Lord Mayor of Cologne, he was a member, as the most civilised parliamentary body he had ever known). But in general, the Prussian conservatives had things their own way in Prussia, and they were not very forthcoming as regards trade unions, social democrats, Catholics and Poles. Right to the very end of the First World War, when the Reich government itself was desperate to show the victorious Americans that Germany could be properly democratic, universal suffrage and all, the Prussian conservatives held out. In fact the *Herrenhaus* only passed an equal-suffrage law, even then with reservations, on the day the Kaiser abdicated.

But the safely Prussian-conservative world which the three-class franchise was supposed to preserve was not in fact preserved at all. The 1880s – Reck-Malleczewen's childhood years – happened. Berlin boomed; vast fortunes shot up from industry and building, rather than from agriculture; the Counts Stolberg-Wernigerode, the only Counts in Germany who had the right to a sovereign's address, sold up their palace just beyond the Brandenburg Gate to the man-on-the-make who created the Hotel Adlon (which, in 1945, became a field hospital, though it was still punctiliously serving drinks to what was left of the diplomatic corps – Croats, Irish etc. – when the Russians were in the Prussian Finance Ministry, a few hundred yards away).

The three-class franchise was subverted, because the Prussian conservatives were easily outweighed by new money, a great deal of it Jewish. In the very centre of Berlin, the constituency *Vossstrasse*, the top third of the tax-payers consisted indeed of one man – the Jewish owner of a vast department store, Wertheimer. Imperial Chancellors, chiefs of the General Staff and the like found themselves in the second class. True, the Prussian conservatives could always rely on a block of seats, about a third, because they could always summon the tenantry, with whom their relations were generally good. But the future was not theirs, and where was a bright young sprig of the old *rocher de bronze* to turn? Some – Counts Westarp and Reventlow – said: let us strive for an English miracle, a popular conservative party: a good idea, but in Germany, unworkable for reasons that preoccupy historians to this day (the best book remains David Blackbourn's *German Sonderweg*, which understands the Catholic dimension of the problem). Others became ardent nationalists, dying in the First World War in enormous numbers. A few took up an *au-dessus-de-la-mêlée* aestheticism, and the poet Stephan George, who had been hugely influential among educated Prussians before 1914, simply walked away from the nationalist passions of 1914, for which he had been to some degree responsible, and went to Switzerland. Later on, after the defeat in 1918 and the crash of old Prussia, this class began to disintegrate. One Reventlow became a Nazi; another joined the Communist party and fought in the Spanish Civil War; a Countess von Malzahn was the most resourceful helper of fugitive Jews during wartime Berlin that there was; one von der Schulenburg tried to blow up Hitler, and even in November 1944 most of the other von der Schulenburgs clubbed together to present to Hitler a fine vellum-and-velvet production containing all of their signatures on the occasion of his miraculous survival.

Hitler was in fact the nemesis of that class. During the 1920s, when Germany, rather at bayonet-point, tried democracy (i.e. universal, equal – indeed relentless – suffrage with proportional representation at its most grotesquely literal-minded), the conservatives had not behaved constructively. What struck me about Reck-Malleczewen's diaries is the Catholic connection. There is much background to this.

Bismarck had felt he could manage Catholics. His conservative opponents in Prussia just did not want Catholics at all: they were prone to demagogy, bred like rabbits, ran up debts, and somehow understood democracy rather better than honest Lutherans did. Max Weber's famous book, *The Protestant Ethic and the Spirit of Capitalism*, written (in about six weeks) in 1903, is a testimony to this. This attitude survives between North and South Germany (a German officer remarked to me, as we went on a pub-crawl round Tallinn a few years ago, gloomily: 'What a pity it wasn't a sixty years' war'), but it is only a bare shadow of what it used to be. Lutheran and Catholic were forced into alliance, after the Second

World War, and West Germany became increasingly Catholic-dominated as time went by, while Lutheranism shrivelled. Even in the German officers' corps nowadays, you are as likely to hear soft, lilting Bavarian or Rhenish accents as *schnoddrig* tones from that barrack-room North German sand-box.

Intriguing then, given Reck-Malleczewen's Protestant, North German, conservative background, that his friends in this diary are Catholic. Another interesting thing is that, though in Prussia the only really active resistance to the Nazis came from the upper classes, the Catholic masses in southern Germany were, if not actively resistant, far less enthusiastic about the Nazis than the North German masses ever were. This, perhaps, takes some explaining.

Reck-Malleczewen, moving to wartime Bavaria (where, there being a higher proportion of peasants than in the rest of Germany, and a great many tucked-away villages, you could, apart from anything else, eat rather better), knew, socially, quite a number of the local Catholic big-wigs. He refers even to the royal family, the Wittelsbachs – and they were always anti-Nazi, to the point of emigration (to Hungary, which was safely Catholic conservative at the time). Prinz Rupprecht, who had commanded an army group against the British in France in 1918, was a focus for resistance. Once parliamentary democracy came in – Bavaria got a form of universal suffrage earlier than elsewhere in Germany – the parliament in Munich was dominated by Catholic machines, associated with the *Zentrums-partei*, the word *Zentrum* meaning, more or less, 'focus' in this case for Catholics to defend their interests. Catholics even preferred social democrats to the stiff-necked Protestant worthies who would otherwise have run things, and they did, locally, some interesting deals. When public transport was organised, the Catholics supplied the bus-conductors, the social democrats the drivers. Public offices, at a low level, could be shared out in the same way, and even unnecessarily multiplied. Who paid? Why, the better-off urban Protestant tax-payer, of course. A form of municipal politics, which bedevilled many advanced countries in western Europe thereafter, and which led, in the case of this country, to the Poll Tax, thus emerged. Once finances and debts became fouled up with inflation and the loss of the First World War, Bavarian Protestants turned ugly. It was among them that Hitler took his Bavarian votes. Peculiarly enough, Hitler himself, and his propaganda minister, Goebbels, were lapsed Catholics. The rest were overwhelmingly Protestant in origin, and throughout Germany Protestants were far more likely to vote Nazi than Catholics were.

Reck-Malleczewen, a Prussian nobleman, has the attitudes of his class, despising the plebeian Nazis. Again and again, it is their vulgarity that repels him, and he must have made his attitudes perfectly plain, since the Gestapo arrested and executed him in the end. Here he is, with his well-cut English clothes, from Savile Row, having to put up with what Orwell called 'shiny-bottomed bureaucrats and gunmen' in a vermin-infested cell, while the sons of his friends are slaughtered in Hitler's absurd war, the coffee tastes of mud, and the clothes are so heavily made up of timber that when you clap someone on the shoulder, there is a hollow thud. The newspapers lie, sweaty little men in brown shirts strut, and ghastly things happen (though mainly off-stage in the diaries) to the Jews. Reck-Malleczewen, who has taken his pessimism from the classics, transmitted via Spengler, despairs, but does so loudly. He also notes something hopeful: that the Bavarian population around are not quite so loyally crazy as their Nazi masters would have liked. For instance, when the Allies landed in North Africa, in November 1942, the Bavarians began to take stock. That month, an Anglo-American armada invaded Morocco, and quite rapidly took control of French North Africa. Reck-Malleczewen cheers, and notes the patriotic enthusiasms of the Bavarian to undergo change. People are already thinking of their post-war positions and reputation; they begin not to notice this, and to connive at that. If you read the multi-volume series, *The Resistance to National Socialism in Bavaria*, produced in the 1960s, your first reaction is disbelief. Resistance? Bavaria? German friends of mine have sniffed: just some tax-evasion, some illegal pig-slaughtering. In practice, the fate of the Scholls, brother and sister, executed in 1943 for launching anti-Nazi leaflets in Munich, was not as untypical as all that. Experience in other countries showed that sabotage to the Nazi war-effort was more effective than outright resistance, and the Bavarians were not keen Nazis, whatever their defects, otherwise. I found Reck-Malleczewen's account of this changing mood the most interesting part of the diaries, but there is competition from other aspects.

Unfortunately, the contempt for the *canaille*, by Reck-Malleczewen's equivalents had amounted to a sort of self-fulfilling prophecy. The German conservative party, turned, after 1918, into the German National People's Party, took, at one stage, almost a quarter of the vote, and thus became, in politics, king-maker. Collaborating, as its elements did after 1949, with other parties for the maintenance of the rule of law, it could have maintained German parliamentary democracy. A few people apart, it did not do so. It said: let democracy collapse, and we shall inherit. It therefore let Hitler happen, never supposing that this vulgarian would get out of control: 'we have hired him' (as you would a servant) said the preposterous von Papen. But Hitler speedily out-manoeuvred them, and their party was closed down, in June 1934, while von Papen narrowly escaped assassination. There was an irony in Reck-Malleczewen's landing in Catholic Bavaria, immolated at the hands of, of all things, a lapsed Austrian Catholic.

Germany did indeed rise again. Some of the Right – academic, *bürgerlich*, types, for the most part – looked at the Nazis and saw in them a socialist, state-control affair. The answer for the next German state must therefore be of a free-marketing kind. The economics for this were established by experts such as Ludwig Erhard, working in internal emigration under an industrialist's protection for the war years. Against much opposition, even from the occupying forces' authorities (particularly the British), he produced, by stealth, a hard currency, the *Deutsche Mark*, in June 1948, and the economic miracle got under way: even in 1951. Germany was exporting more than the British. But there were others who saw that economic formulae, however up-to-date and ingenious, were not enough. The free market would have to be underpinned, constitutionally, by protection for the basic things that mattered. Children must be properly looked after, and the family, therefore, given some guarantees. Into the Basic Law was written a provision, for instance, that no father of a family must be taxed to below the level at which he could decently keep his family.

These, and similar, arguments amounted to a moral extension of the classical liberalism of the economists. The men who had these things worked out – Wilhelm Röpke, Alexander Röntgen, Friedrich von Hayek and others – had their own journal, *Ordo*, which was extremely influential in the making of the German Federal Republic. Quite a number of them, out of disgust for the Nazis, though they were not Jewish or Communist, simply took the road into exile. Curiously enough, several of them had years and years of experience in Atatürk's Turkey, where a fascinating experiment in state-building was being conducted, in terrain that looked at first sight rather unpropitious. Their influence in Turkey is still remembered with pride and affection. After the war, they were able to talk to Catholics of the generation that followed old Adenauer, in a way that, in the heyday of Prussian conservatism, would have been more or less unthinkable. Back in those times, Prussian conservatives and Bavarian Catholics might collaborate, at Reich level, in what was called 'the blue-black block' to arrange such matters as pig-prices, but they did not, otherwise, like each other at all.

Reck-Malleczewen was not, of course, a classical liberal. But he himself was obviously coming round to the idea that, pessimistic though he might be, he had something in common with Bavarian

Catholics. His diaries are, if you like, a kind of black-humour and far-off counterpoint to the themes of the *Ordoliberalen*. What would he have made of the Germany of today, after unification, this time, at the hands of the Rhineland Catholic, Dr Kohl? For that is the summation of his diaries, and not, despite the endless gloom which sometimes pervades Germans, altogether a bad outcome after all.

Translator's Preface

This book is history of a kind that will be found in few history books. It is, in the real sense of the word, *living* history, because it is the history of Germany in the Nazi period as was experienced by an extremely vital and aware man, Friedrich Percyval Reck-Malleczewen.

This is the accurate account of the forebodings of Reck-Malleczewen, who put his thoughts down as the only means of defending himself from a horror that finally engulfed him. Its entries cease with October 1944, because Reck-Malleczewen was killed by a *Genickschuss*, a shot in the neck, the following 16 February, in the Dachau concentration camp.

When the author began this journal, he was fifty-two, and therefore well into middle-age. And yet what is so extraordinary here is the *power* of the personality that emerges – his vitality, his immense passion. The writer has had 'certain experiences, and looked into certain depths', as he says, and yet even in despair he remains a full-blooded man of powerful commitment. This is the real importance of the book: that a man who stood solidly on the soil of Bavaria looked on as millions of his fellow countrymen became automatons, moving and yelling and salivating to order, and set down what it was to be a full human being among these walking machines.

He set this down so well that we can feel it now, his horror and loneliness, and we know that his feeling is a feeling we ourselves have had, because it belongs to our time – it is the feeling of *our* time that Reck-Malleczewen is describing. And therein lies the true horror.

Fritz Reck – born Friedrich Percyval Reck-Malleczewen, in 1884, the son of an East Prussian Protestant Junker family – was a prophet. He belongs with his great hero, Dostoyevsky, and with Kafka, and with George Orwell, of whom he probably never heard, among that vision-afflicted little band who saw, with Dostoyevsky, that 'the end of the world is at hand,' because men and women no longer knew they had a centre, could no longer hear what it said, could now only continue to move about the earth by various tricks of the mind or body.

Does it seem presumptuous to put Reck-Malleczewen among these other great men on the basis of a single journal, the only work of note he is known to have written, except, perhaps, for a half-completed philosophical work (*Das Ende der Termiten, – The End of the Termites*)? I don't think so. One work is enough. Aldous Huxley is likely to be remembered mainly for *Brave New World*, and Orwell's *1984* will still be read when his other books are forgotten.

Very simply, the problem Reck-Malleczewen faced is our problem – the problem of mass-man.

'Suppose they go on,' he wrote, 'clinging like grapes to the trolleys morning and evening,' and 'charging into the restaurants after ration-free food like the apes at feeding time at the zoo.' He was describing the Munich version of mass-man, circa 1944.... But mass-man *has* gone on. He is with us today.

Of course, Reck-Malleczewen could hardly have conceived this possibility. Mass-man had come to ascendancy in Nazi Germany in such instability, in such conditions of chaos and upheaval that he would certainly, Reck felt, burst like a boil or a bullfrog together with his Nazi state. Fritz Reck could not imagine that any world was fit for inhabiting in which any form of the mass species, fascist or democratic, was dominant. All the hope, the immense passion that underlie this book were based on this: that mass-man would go as the Nazis went.

It did not happen. The physical destruction happened, as he expected. He tells about some of it – the bombing of Hamburg, and of Munich, the sealed freight cars in the sun of a siding amidst the waving grass of Upper Bavaria, with the urine and faeces dripping down onto the track ties from the Russian prisoners of war stuffed inside, the burning, and the destruction. But the Nazi massmen never lost their heads. They killed to the end, ferociously, coldly, unbelievably. They remained incredible, and neither then nor afterward did they ever lose their tight hold on themselves.

And so we did not have that emptying of a boil of corruption that Reck-Malleczewen looked to with such dread and with such hope to save his beloved Germany, and with it the rest of us. Germany lost the war, but mass-man remained.

He is still with us. Look around you. Look into yourself.

A few sections in this book seem inordinately difficult to follow. The phrasing – which could not, I felt, be rendered into simpler English without losing some of the quality of the original – becomes difficult at times. There are references to people and events immediately recognisable only to the highly educated German. When a feeling of overwhelming helplessness strikes a man, as it must often have struck Reck-Malleczewen, he is likely to vent his rage – if he has the vast culture of this man – in turgid phrasing, in obscure and nearly private references. These matters have been explained wherever it was possible to do so, and when this was impossible – the obscurity was left as it is. The book and therefore Reck-Malleczewen, and therefore Germany and what happened to it, can be understood only as a whole, with all the contrarities, confusions, and even spitefulness of the living organism.

Reference to this journal – first published in 1947 in Germany and reissued there in 1966 – by Hannah Arendt in her *Eichmann in Jerusalem: A Report on the Banality of Evil* brought me to read, and then to translate into English for the first time, this book. I felt, and still feel, that the parallels between that time and this one are more sharply expressed, etched more clearly by the heat of this man's passion in this volume than in any other that I know.

I thank my wife, Donna Rubens, my sister, Mary Lou Kallman, and my friend Paul Nardi for their great help to me in completing this book.

Paul Rubens
New York City, January 1970

May 1936

Spengler is dead, then. And just as a deceased maharajah has the right to have all his retainers buried with him, this preponderant personality was, a few days later, followed in death by Albers, who had handled his work at the Beck publishing firm. Albers died in a truly grisly fashion. He threw himself under the wheels of the Starnberg train, and his bloody corpse was found on the tracks, legs severed at the thighs.[1]

As for Spengler, our last meeting was just a few weeks ago on Bayerstrasse, in Munich. As usual, he had been attired in expensive tweeds. As usual, too, his brow had been dark, and his tone angry; his deep hurt and thirst for revenge on those who had hurt him emerged in a series of striking prognoses. It had been worth one's while to spend time with him.

I still remember our first meeting, when Albers brought him to my house. On the little carriage which carried him from the station, and which was hardly built with such loads in mind, sat a massive figure who appeared even more enormous by virtue of the thick overcoat he wore. Everything about him had the effect of extraordinary permanence and solidity: the deep bass voice; the tweed jacket, already, at that time, almost habitual; the appetite at dinner; and at night, the truly Cyclopean snoring, loud as a series of buzz saws, which frightened the other guests at my Chiemgau country house out of their peaceful slumbers.

This was at a time when he was not really successful, and before he had done an about-face and marched into the camp of the oligarchy of industrial magnates, a retreat which determined his life from then on. It was a time when he was still capable of being gay and unpreoccupied, and when he could sometimes even be persuaded to venture forth in all his dignity for a swim in the river. Later, of course, it was unthinkable that he expose himself in his bathing suit before ploughing peasants and farmhands, or that he climb, a huffing and puffing Triton, back onto the river bank in their presence!

He was the strangest amalgam of truly human greatness and small and large frailties that I have ever encountered. If I recall the latter now, it is part of my taking leave of him, and so I am sure it will not be held against me. He was the kind of man who likes to eat alone – a melancholy-eyed feaster at a great orgy of eating. With a certain amusement, I recall one evening when he joined Albers and me for a light supper. It was during the final weeks of the First World War, when there was not a great deal one could set before one's guests. But, discoursing and declaiming the whole time, Spengler finished an entire goose without leaving us, his table companions, so much as a bite.

His passion for huge dinners (the check for which was later picked up by his industrial Maecenas) was not his only diverting attribute. After I had met him, still before his first major success, he asked me not to come to visit him at his little apartment (I believe it was on Agnesstrasse,[2] in Munich). The reason he gave was that his apartment was too confined, and he wanted to show me his library in surroundings appropriate to its monumental scope.

Then, in 1926, after he had found his way to the mighty rulers of heavy industry[3] and had moved to expensive Widenmayerstrasse on the banks of the Isar, he did, indeed, invite me to see the succession of huge rooms in his apartment there. He showed me his carpets and paintings, and even his bed – which was truly worth seeing, because it looked more like a catafalque – but he became visibly disconcerted when I said that I was still looking forward to seeing the library. After overcoming his reluctance to show it to me, I found myself in a rather small room. And there – on a well-battered walnut bookstand, alongside a row of Ullstein books and detective stories – stood what are commonly called 'dirty books'.

But I have never known a man with so little sense of humour and such sensitivity to even the smallest criticism. There was nothing he abhorred so much as humbug; yet along with all the magnificent deductions in *The Decline of the West*, he allowed a host of inaccuracies, inadvertencies, and actual errors to stand uncorrected – such as that Dostoyevsky came into the world in St Petersburg rather than in Moscow, and that Duke Bernhard of Weimar died *before* Wallenstein was assassinated – and important conclusions were drawn from these errors. Mistakes like these could happen to anyone; but woe to the man who dared make Spengler aware of them!

I remember a delightful scene which took place at my house, when, as was his custom after dinner, he fell to lecturing and preaching at the same time that he catechised a follower of his who was present. What was amusing was that this proselyte, who was just back from Africa where he had caught a severe case of malaria, had fallen asleep and was snoring very loudly in his armchair; but between one snore and the next, by the principle of automatic response to 'his Master's voice', he promptly answered, in faultless Spenglerian jargon, every question put to him by the great man. Spengler, the Master, might well have been pleased, and he certainly should have been able to laugh at this incident. Instead, he was deeply hurt, and would have nothing to do with the culprit thereafter.

To repeat, he was truly the most humourless man I have ever met; in this respect, he is surpassed only by Herr Hitler and his Nazis, who have every prospect of dying of a wretchedness compounded by their own deep-rooted humourlessness and the dreary monotony of public life which, under their domination, has taken on the rigidity of a corpse and is now in its fourth year of suffocating us to death. But he who believes that I want to do Spengler an injury by recounting his many weaknesses is in error. I need not cite his indispensable early work on Theocrates,[4] nor the fact that he gave form at last to the presentiments of an entire generation. Whoever has met him knows about the nimbus of the significant that attached to him and that was not dissipated even in his off-guard moments; knows that in him lived on the representation of the best in humanist pedagogy; knows about his countenance, which reflected the same stoicism found in busts of the late Roman period.

As to whether or not he ever perceived the rising of the irrational on the horizon of our existence where it can now be seen, whether he sensed that the 'decline of the West' announced by him was actually only the decline of the world created by Renaissance man in the last four hundred years – this I do not know. For it was his destiny that midway in his course he fell into dependency on the heavy-industry oligarchy, and this dependency began in time to have an effect on his thinking. I, at least, with the best will in the world, do not otherwise know how to reconcile the truly magnificent prophesying of the approaching Dostoyevskian Christianity, made in 1922 in the second volume of *Decline*, with the technocratic rhetoric which fills his later work. It was his tragedy that a highly intellectualised, and I might say, a seedy-teacher kind of negativity, kept him from believing in the gods, much less in God. His followers began to leave him around 1926, when he made his peace with contemporary Germany – not with the Nazis, for I know of no one who hated them as he did, on lying down, in sleeping, and in rising up! – but with those businessmen-on-horseback from the Ruhr, who made themselves the real masters of the state following the downfall of the monarchy and who were more than happy to satisfy Spengler's longing for a lifestyle that was patrician as well as somewhat hedonistic. The surging power of his mind, to which we owe the vision of his early works, was cut off from the time the ravens – not those of St Anthony, but those of the Messrs

Thyssen and Hösch – began to supply his table with good burgundies.

Thus was he betrayed by his own epicurean inclinations and his passion for the rich sauces and incomparable culinary skill of his sisters, who kept house for him. The Nazis – in their so-called newspapers edited by such people as one-time schoolteachers with peculiar records and army lieutenants of the First World War who have done nothing since – are exulting over the fact that Spengler supposedly came around to their way of thinking; they are also saying that, one by one, the same thing is happening to the rest of the opposition. But the second, unpublished volume of Spengler's *Years of Decision*, the first volume of which nearly made him a martyr, lies safely stored in a bank vault in Switzerland,[5] awaiting the resurrection toward which all our hopes turn.

July 1936

From Munich – now appearing almost foreign – from Prussian-occupied Munich, comes an amusing tale. It concerns Herr Esser,[6] the Minister of Transport, who, in view of his known activities, should really be called the Minister of Sexual Transports. This Esser had an affair with the daughter of the owner of a tavern, and was so badly beaten by the father that he could neither go out nor, compromised as he was, remain in Munich. In accordance with the style of this regime, which has simply discarded decency as so much excess baggage, he was promoted shortly thereafter to a much higher post in Berlin. From there, he has just announced that travelling abroad by an individual has now become a thing of the past, and that henceforth a German can leave his country only as part of a herd, the 'Strength Through Joy' organisation. We have, therefore, every prospect of losing whatever remains of our freedom of movement, and of thus becoming completely the prisoners of this horde of vicious apes who three years ago seized power over us.

I had a most enlightening talk recently with a man about the Nazis, and how they had come to power. He said that this so-called German Revolution[7] is really based on simple blackmail. This is his story.

Old Hindenburg had always been a poor man. He decided near the end to change that situation, and he had his son, Oskar, take over his business affairs. Oskar speculated on the stock exchange, and when the crash came suddenly, owed 13 million marks. To make this back, Oskar then let himself get involved in the Eastern Relief manipulations – I do not believe his father knew – and the

Nazis found out in 1932. (The fall of the Brüning Cabinet is very likely connected.) The Hitlerites got photostats of the incriminating documents, and from then on had the whip hand.

Hindenburg had always before that kept Hitler away. He may well have said that 'I wouldn't make that Bohemian[8] corporal Postmaster, much less Chancellor,' as reported. But by the summer of 1932, he was no longer a free agent. Otherwise how could he, the Chief of State, have said absolutely nothing when Hitler had the effrontery to send a telegram congratulating the Nazi murderers at Potempa?[9]

At the end of 1932, questions in the Reichstag about the Eastern Relief boondoggle began to touch on Hindenburg's Neudeck estate. The Hindenburg group began to be very worried. Then came the Berlin strike,[10] to make the people in von Papen's cabinet more amenable to the Nazi 'solution'. Hitler felt that he could now press to be named Chancellor.

The story dovetails perfectly with information I have from other sources. Gregor Strasser,[11] who was killed in the Röhm Putsch, hinted something of the same thing to me in November 1932. This also explains the secret conferences at von Papen's villa between the Hindenburg group and the Nazis. Frau von Schröter[12] acted as mediator at these talks, and von Papen, who had been trembling for the safety of his wife's fortune ever since the Transport Strike, played a strange role at them.

And this explains, finally, the report, which keeps cropping up despite every denial, that von Schleicher,[13] who was on the other side in this intrigue, had Oskar von Hindenburg arrested at the Friedrichstrasse railroad station, and held overnight, following the break with the old President. General von Bredow, who was killed along with Schleicher in the Röhm Putsch a year and a half later, reportedly was the arresting officer.

So it seems that we owe the unutterable misery into which we have come to blackmail and to a financial lapse of Paul von Hindenburg.

I am not in a position to be judge of a dead man. I consider that his lack of decision when the monarchy was threatened, on 9 November 1918, was treason to the Crown. The story about his deathbed encounter[14] with Hitler has given me a great deal of food for thought.

Hindenburg refused to have Hitler come to his bedside. But Hitler was not to be put off that way: his prestige was at stake. He forced his way in, and got his blessing. Hindenburg had never forgiven himself for his betrayal of the Kaiser sixteen years before. He evidently confused Hitler with the Kaiser, stroked his hand, and *begged him to forgive him.*

If even a small part of all this is true, the truth, when it emerges, will shake the country. I am not concerned about the old man's image: Old Hindenburg simply was unable to measure up to the situation. I do not believe he was capable of doing anything wrong, with all his faculties. And it may well be that his slowness to react, during the First World War, often saved a battle that Ludendorff's wildly pragmatic manoeuvring was about to lose.

General Hoffmann[15] was an aide, and his widow recently showed me a letter her husband had written her in the fall of 1914, just before the German advance through northern Poland. It read: 'He [Hoffmann meant Hindenburg] spends most of the time hunting, gets back to headquarters at night, has next day's order read off to him, and says: "Begad, fellas, I couldn't do any better myself!" Herr von Bethmann-Hollweg will be coming for a briefing on the strategic situation. We will have to tell the General what to think. He does not even know where his troops are stationed.'

I repeat, I am not going to judge a dead man. Hindenburg did not have the stature for the position he was given. He was also too old, and very likely too sick to handle it. But the stupidity of an entire people in agreeing to this combination of corruption and inadequacy in its leadership is something else again. The cabinet system is responsible, too: as long as this country agrees to that political institution, it will have to bear the confusion, convulsions, and political mayhem which accompany it. No, the Germans as they now are need a master. And by this I most certainly do not mean that forelocked gypsy type we have been given to lead us in our hour of need.

11 August 1936

Met Frankenberg in Munich, and we talked about the Röhm Putsch. Röhm died bravely, as a soldier should, after registering a complaint about the quality of the coffee served in prison. The version disseminated by Goebbels and his underlings, that he hid under the bed, is one more lie, the kind of vicious, cowardly slander of a man no longer alive to answer it, in which they specialise. It will come back on their own heads some day, all of it.

Then, there is the case of Willi Schmid,[16] the music critic for a Munich newspaper, who was killed in the Putsch through over-sight – you might say, unfortunate confusion of identity. It seems that the Nazis, looking for *their* Schmid in the telephone book, killed a whole column of Schmids before they got to the one they wanted. This is known as being 'better safe than sorry'. Seventy-two-year-old Gustav von Kahr[17] was not shot; he was trampled to death by the SS in the courtyard of the Hotel Marienbad.

The whole thing, the entire Röhm Putsch, is strange, full of unfathomable ramifications; when the whole truth comes out some day, it will make people shudder....I understand that Hitler himself took on the job of killing some of his enemies in the course of his Apache-style raid on Bad Wiessee,[18] and that one of his intended victims fought back. Bellowing with rage, brandishing his pistol, he chased his Führer downstairs to the basement, where Hitler finally found refuge behind an iron-sheathed door. Lovely Hamlet-like beginning for our new regime, promising all kinds of pleasantness to follow!

I have been working on my book about the Münster city-state

set up by the Anabaptist heretics in the sixteenth century. I read accounts of this 'Kingdom of Zion' by contemporaries, and I am shaken. In every respect, down to the most ridiculous details, that was a forerunner of what we are now enduring. Like the Germany of today, the Münster city-state for years separated itself from the civilised world; like Nazi Germany, it was hugely successful over a long period of time, and appeared invincible. And then, suddenly, against all expectation and over a comparative trifle it collapsed....

As in our case, a misbegotten failure conceived, so to speak, in the gutter, became the great prophet, and the opposition simply disintegrated, while the rest of the world looked on in astonishment and incomprehension. As with us (for in Berchtesgaden, recently, crazed women swallowed the gravel on which our handsome gypsy of a leader had set his foot), hysterical females, schoolmasters, renegade priests, the dregs and outsiders from everywhere formed the main supports of the regime. I have to delete some of the parallels in order not to jeopardise myself any more than I already have. A thin sauce of ideology covered lewdness, greed, sadism, and fathomless lust for power, in Münster, too, and whoever would not completely accept the new teaching was turned over to the executioner. The same role of official murderer played by Hitler in the Röhm Putsch was acted by Bockelson in Münster. As with us, Spartan laws were promulgated to control the *misera plebs*, but these did not apply to him and his followers. Bockelson also surrounded himself with bodyguards, and was beyond the reach of any would-be assassin. As with us, there were street meetings and 'voluntary contributions', refusal of which meant proscription. As with us, the masses were drugged: folk festivals, useless construction, anything and everything, to keep the man in the street from a moment's pause to reflect.

Exactly as Nazi Germany has done, Münster sent its fifth columns and prophets forth to undermine neighbouring states. The fact that the Münster propaganda chief, Dusentschnur, limped like Goebbels is a joke which history spent four hundred years preparing: a fact which I, familiar as I am with the vindictiveness of our Minister of Lies, have most advisedly omitted in my book. Constructed on a foundation of lies, there existed for a short time between the Middle Ages and modern times a bandits' regime. It threatened all the established world – Kaiser, nobility, and all the old relationships. And it was all designed to still the hunger for mastery of a couple of power-mad thugs. A few things have yet to happen to complete the parallel. In the besieged Münster of 1534, the people were driven to swallow their own excrement, to eat their own children. This could happen to us too, just as Hitler and his sycophants face the same inevitable end as Bockelson and Knipperdolling.

I stand before these 400-year-old records, startled by the thought that the resemblance may not be coincidence at all, but may be determined by some frightful law decreeing periodic draining of a psychic abscess. How much do we really know about the vaults and caverns which lie somewhere under the structure of a great nation – about these psychic catacombs in which all our concealed desires, our fearful dreams and evil spirits, our vices and our forgotten and unexpiated sins, have been buried for generations? In healthy times, these emerge as the spectres in our dreams. To the artist they appear as Satanic apparitions. Then, on our cathedrals, the Gothic gargoyles push obscene backsides out into the air, and there creep across the inspired canvases of Grünewald, with beaked nose and claw-foot, the representations of all the vices; those flagellants strike at the Saviour so that the law may be fulfilled, and in the very inevitability of it one feels pity....

But suppose, now, that all of these things generally kept buried in our subconscious were to drive for emergence in the blood-cleansing function of a boil? Suppose that this underworld now and again liberated by Satan bursts forth, and the evil spirits escape the Pandora's box? Isn't this exactly what happened in Münster, so conservative before and after the event? Doesn't this explain how all of this could have happened to a basically orderly and hard-working people, without resistance from those dedicated to the good in life, in the same kind of grim and incalculably vast cosmic convulsion which from the first day of the Hitler regime has not only brought sunspots to affect the weather, endlessly rainy summers to spoil the harvests, and strange crawling things to afflict this old earth, but has also in some unfathomable way turned on its head concepts like mine and thine, right and wrong, virtue and vice, God and the Devil?

I happened to be in Munich recently, just as one of the official festivals, which are by now an everyday occurrence, was being celebrated to the blare of tubas and the rat-tat of drums. I could not get a room at my usual hotel near the station, and found a place to sleep in the Old City, opposite a schoolhouse in which a visiting Hitler Youth troop had been lodged for the holiday period.

I saw one of these boys, who had just thrown off his knapsack, look about him at the empty classroom, I observed how his glance fell on the crucifix hanging behind the teacher's desk, how in an instant this young and still soft face contorted in fury, how he ripped this symbol, to which the cathedrals of Germany, and the ringing progressions of the *St Matthew Passion* are consecrated, off the wall and threw it out of the window into the street....

With the cry: 'Lie there, you dirty Jew!'

I have seen this. Among people I know, I have heard of more than one case of children denouncing their parents politically, and thereby delivering them to the axe. Ah, I do not believe that all these children are born devils: yesterday, that Christ-killer may well have been entranced by the fairy tale about the juniper tree, or the one about faithful Heinrich, around whose heart, in his loyalty and his concern over his bewitched and banished master, there grew an iron band.

My life in this pit will soon enter its fifth year. For more than forty-two months, I have thought hate, have lain down with hate in my heart, have dreamed hate and awakened with hate. I suffocate in the knowledge that I am the prisoner of a horde of vicious apes, and I rack my brains over the perpetual riddle of how this same people which so jealously watched over its rights a few years ago can have sunk into this stupor, in which it not only allows itself to be dominated by the street-corner idlers of yesterday, but actually, height of shame, is *incapable any longer of perceiving its shame for the shame that it is.*

I saw Hitler last in Seebruck, slowly gliding by in a car with armour-plated sides, while an armed bodyguard of motorcyclists rode in front as further protection: a jellylike, slag-gray face, a moonface into which two melancholy jet-black eyes had been set like raisins. So sad, so unutterably insignificant, so basically misbegotten is this countenance that only thirty years ago, in the darkest days of Wilhelmism, such a face on an official would have been impossible. Appearing in the chair of a minister, an apparition with a face like this would have been disobeyed as soon as its mouth spoke an order – and not merely by the higher officials in the ministry: no, by the doorman, by the cleaning women!

And today? I hear that Hitler recently ended a report – by Wilhelm Keitel, the Army commander – which had given him reason for dissatisfaction, by throwing a bronze vase at the head of the general. Isn't this the kind of thing that happens when a people is sinking in the cesspool of its own disgrace? 'And all that they did was as it should have been, because it was God's will.' This I read in a sixteenth-century Münster chronicle.

I am neither an occult nor a mystic. I am a child of my time despite all forebodings, and I hold strictly to what I see. But there is a frightful riddle here, and I come back again and again to what appears to me to be the only answer to it:

What I saw gliding by there, behind the fence of his mamelukes, like the Prince of Darkness himself, was no human being.

That was a figure out of a ghost story.

I have met him a few times – not at any of his meetings, of

course. The first time was in 1920, at the home of my friend
Clemens von Franckenstein,[19] which was then the Lenbach villa.
According to the butler, one of those present was forcing his way
in everywhere, had already been there a full hour. It was Hitler. He
had managed an invitation to Clé's house under the guise of being
interested in operatic scenic design. (Clé had been general inten-
dant of the Royal Theatre.) Hitler very likely had the idea that
theatrical design was connected with interior decorating and wall-
paper-hanging, his former profession.

He had come to a house, where he had never been before,
wearing gaiters, a floppy, wide-brimmed hat, and carrying a riding
whip. There was a collie too. The effect, among the Gobelin tapestries and cool marble walls, was something akin to a cowboy's
sitting down on the steps of a baroque altar in leather breeches,
spurs, and with a Colt at his side. But Hitler sat there, the stereo-
type of a headwaiter – at that time he was thinner, and looked
somewhat starved – both impressed and restricted by the presence
of a real, live Herr Baron; awed, not quite daring to sit fully in his
chair, but perched on half, more or less, of his thin loins; not
caring at all that there was a great deal of cool and elegant irony
in the things his host said to him, but snatching hungrily at the
words, like a dog at pieces of raw meat.

Eventually, he managed to launch into a speech. He talked on
and on, endlessly. He preached. He went on at us like a division
chaplain in the Army. We did not in the least contradict him, or
venture to differ in any way, but he began to bellow at us. The
servants thought we were being attacked, and rushed in to defend
us.

When he had gone, we sat silently confused and not at all
amused. There was a feeling of dismay, as when on a train you
suddenly find you are sharing a compartment with a psychotic. We
sat a long time and no one spoke. Finally, Clé stood up, opened
one of the huge windows, and let the spring air, warm with the
föhn, into the room. It was not that our grim guest had been

unclean, and had fouled the room in the way that so often happens in a Bavarian village. But the fresh air helped to dispel the feeling of oppression. It was not that an unclean body had been in the room, but something else: the unclean essence of a monstrosity.

I used to ride at the Munich armoury, after which I liked to eat at the Löwenbräukeller: that was the second meeting. He did not need to worry now that he might be put out, and so he did not have to smack his boots continually with his riding whip, as he had done at Franckenstein's. At first glance, the tightly clenched insecurity seemed to be gone – which allowed him to launch at once into one of his tirades. I had ridden hard, and was tremendously hungry, and wanted just to be let alone to eat in peace. Instead I had poured out over me every one of the political platitudes in his book. I know you will appreciate my sparing you, future reader, all the dogma. It was that little-man Machiavellianism by which German foreign policy became a series of legalised burglaries and the activity of its leaders a succession of embezzlements, forgeries, and treaty breaches, all designed to make him appeal to the assortment of schoolteachers, bureaucrats, and stenographers who have since become the true support and bastion of his regime ... as a fabulous fellow, a real political Genghis Khan.

With his oily hair falling into his face as he ranted, he had the look of a man trying to seduce the cook. I got the impression of basic *stupidity*, the same kind of stupidity as that of his crony, Papen – the kind of stupidity which equates statesmanship with cheating at a horse trade.

But this impression was not the last one I had, nor the most striking. Every time I think about it, I am more and more struck by the way this Machiavelli preaching away at me between my sausage and my veal chop bowed to me when we parted – like a waiter who has just received a fair tip. And this image is like that photograph in which he is shown shaking hands with Hindenburg – the same image of a headwaiter closing his hand around the tip.

The third time, I saw him in a courtroom accused of creating a disturbance at some political meeting: by then, he was known outside the Munich city limits.... And then I observed him in Berlin, entering his hotel, already a celebrity. In court, he looked like he was begging for a kind word from the small and very low-ranking official who was in charge of the hearing: the look of a man who has been in jail a number of times. On the other occasion, he went by the doorman with the stiffened back of a man who is going to ask the hotel manager for credit, and knows he is likely to be thrown out.

Notwithstanding his meteoric rise, there is absolutely nothing that has happened in the twenty years since I first saw him to make me change my first view of him. The fact remains that he was, and is, without the slightest self-awareness and pleasure in himself, that he basically hates himself, and that his opportunism, his immeasurable need for recognition, and his now-apocalyptic vanity are all based on one thing – a consuming drive to drown out the pain in his psyche, the trauma of a monstrosity.

There are additional details – Erna Hanfstaengl, who knows him better than I do, says he is becoming increasingly afraid of ghosts. She believes that this fear of the spirits of those he has murdered drives him on continually, and does not allow him to stay for long in any one place.... Quite in accord with this is that he has taken to spending his nights in his private projection room, where his poor projectionists have to show six films for him, night after night....

This may well be. It only confirms my diagnosis. I do not even believe that the man is especially amoral – the title of great criminal does him too much honour. If a German government had built a gigantic studio, subsidised the newspapers to declare him the greatest artist of all time, and managed to satisfy his limitless vanity that way, I believe he would have turned to completely harmless pursuits and would never have gotten the idea of setting fire to the world.

No, I do not believe in his being a Borgia type. I believe that in this case the offal-compounded, repressed drives of a deeply miscarried human being were combined with a whim of history, which allowed him, as Cleon was once allowed in Athens, to play for a time with the levers of its gigantic machinery. I believe that all of this coincided with a fevered hour of this people. I believe that this poor devil, sprung out of a Strindbergian excremental Hell, like that other time's Bockelson, coincided in time with the bursting of an abscess by a nation, and came as the embodiment of all the dark and generally well-curbed desires of the masses – like his Münster predecessor, a character out of a German ghost story!

I saw him once more at close range. This was in the autumn of 1932, as the fever began to take hold of Germany. Friedrich von Mücke and I were dining at the Osteria Bavaria in Munich when Hitler entered and crossed the restaurant to the table next to ours – alone, by the way, and without his usual bodyguard. There he sat, now a power among the Germans ... sat, felt himself observed by us, and critically examined, and as a result became uncomfortable. His face took on the sullen expression of a minor bureaucrat who has ventured into a place which he would not generally enter, but now that he is there demands for his good money 'that he be served and treated every bit as well as the fine gentlemen over there ...'

There he sat, a raw-vegetable Genghis Khan, a teetotalling Alexander, a womanless Napoleon, an effigy of Bismarck who would certainly have had to go to bed for four weeks if he had ever tried to eat just one of Bismarck's breakfasts....

I had driven into town, and since at that time, September 1932, the streets were already quite unsafe, I had a loaded revolver with me. In the almost deserted restaurant, I could easily have shot him. If I had had an inkling of the role this piece of filth was to play, and of the years of suffering he was to make us endure, I would have done it without a second thought. But I took him for a character out of a comic strip, and did not shoot.

It would have done no good in any case: in the councils of the

Highest, our martyrdom had already been decided. If Hitler at that point had been taken and tied to railroad tracks, the train would have been derailed before it got to him. But when his hour strikes, the end will come down upon his head from every possible direction, and from places, even, that were never thought of. There are many rumours of attempts to assassinate him. The attempts fail, and they will continue to fail. For years (and especially in this land of successful demons) it has seemed that God is asleep. But, to quote a Russian proverb:

'When God wills it, even a broom can shoot!'

May 1937

Reports of a new political scandal have spread across Germany. Putzi Hanfstaengl,[20] scion of the well-known Munich publishing family, and until now *enfant gâté* of Nazidom, has fallen out of favour. It happened quickly. One cold February morning, he boarded a plane ostensibly bound for Spain. In mid-flight, the plane went into a series of loops designed to throw him out of it and when this failed he was set down, in the midst of a swirling snowstorm and with the temperature ten degrees below freezing, somewhere in the forests of Thuringia, and wearing a business suit. He got back to Berlin, and found that his office there – he had been information officer for the entire foreign press – was closed. The English Ambassador, Sir Eric Phipps, who had previously interceded in the Röhm Putsch in favour of Brüning and Treviranus, the Cabinet Minister, helped him get away to England.

The reason for this rather unusual method of obtaining a resignation from office is said to be that Hanfstaengl was much too critical of German intervention in Spain, and also that a film company of his infringed on Goebbels' territory. Another story is that he drank too much in a Paris café, and was overheard talking about a connection between Tukhachevsky and the others now involved in the Moscow trials and Himmler, and that this led to the uncovering of the whole plot. In any case, Hanfstaengl, with whom I dined at the Regina in Munich only a few weeks ago, and whom I consider a man of courtesy and breeding, is now in England. Since he knows the answer to the mystery that surrounds, or is supposed to surround, the burning of the Reichstag,[21] Berlin fears the worst.

Hanfstaengl's eighty-year-old mother has been sent to London to bring him back, carrying with her the *salva guardia* of the German government, and the special guarantee of Herr Göring in default thereof....

In default! The Hanfstaengls are tied to Germany by every economic link, their assets are here, and they are open to whatever action the government may decide to take against them. So the mother went, but the son would not play the game, and declared that he knew exactly how much the word of a Hitler or a Göring was worth. And there this edifying little trifle rests for the moment.

With Herr Arno Rechberg,[22] I breakfasted at the home of Putzi's sister, Erna. Erna hid Hitler after the Nazis' attempted coup at the Feldherrnhalle years ago,[23] and could therefore bear the title of 'Patroness of the Third Reich'. Now, however, the lady is raging at Goebbels, whom she accuses of envy and personal rancour, and charges with an old matter so far known only in broadest outline.

It seems that in the late autumn of 1933, at a time when she was living in an extremely isolated villa east of Munich, on the very edge of suburban Bogenhausen, her house was entered while she was away. She went to Herr Himmler about this, and he later informed her that the entry had been ordered by an official so high up no redress was possible and further that it had not been her letters only they were after, but her life. He therefore declined to have anything further to do with the matter and urged her to move to the centre of town. She followed this advice, and now told me that the official was Herr Goebbels, and that he had ordered the search for the purpose of obtaining certain letters which Hitler had sent her, these letters to be employed in case of emergency – as, for example, the loss of his post and consequent flight abroad – against his lord and master, Hitler.

An amusing story, since our somewhat stunted Great Chief thus supposedly strove for the love of this generously proportioned lady: Erna Hanfstaengl, in contrast to Hitler, represents the typical Munich Bavarian.

Thus we live in Germany today.

With us at Erna Hanfstaengl's was a young Englishwoman, a type somewhere between archangel and model for a toilet soap ad. Her name is Unity Mitford,[24] and her usual perch is atop the Obersalzberg, in the court of Herr Hitler. Her purpose is to become Queen of Germany, with the aim of bringing about reconciliation between Germany and England.

This forceful lady, and Hitler: *Bon Voyage....*

Meantime, I have been in Berlin – Berlin, centre of all diligence, activity, and perfection – by its own statement. In my humble opinion, however, it is like an immense machine, all sound and fury and producing nothing.

I do not believe in any of it. I know all about 'telephoning with both hands and feet', about appointment pads on which every minute for the next three months is scheduled for engagements and 'conferences'. I know all about production-at-any-price, and the desperate hankering after a pseudo Americanism. It is the viewing of all life as a kind of gigantic Army barracks which has brought on us the aversion of the whole world. As long as this country allows itself to be represented by this basically *hopeless* city, we will go from one foreign policy disaster to the next.

I do not believe there is any substance to the idea that people in Berlin work harder than elsewhere. They have a hysterical drive to keep moving, probably an indication of a flight from the knowledge of their own inner emptiness. I believe that it is the same kind of false front trickery that turns the slave-driver of two barmaids into a 'Herr Director', the backyard shack of every housing project into a 'Garden Pavilion', and every discussion on how to cheat a customer on a shipment of dehydrated soup into a 'conference'.

I believe in what really has substance in Berlin, what is productive and really works: the workers of Berlin-East, the streetcar conductors, the mail carriers and the truck drivers. I believe in the taxi driver, like a good and concerned father, who, when I told him the suburb I wanted him to take me to, warned me about the fare for the trip, and in a burst of Prussian thrift advised me to take the elevated.... Oh, I believe in the grumpy soundness of the Berlin concierge, I believe in the kind of humour that placed at the foot of the statue of sabre-waving Blücher:

'There's only room for one on this stove.'[25]

What I do not accept is this disgusting dry rot which has set in here in the last ninety years ... these females with their sunglasses, their yard-wide backsides, and huge bosoms, playing at being ladies ... these Herr Directors with their appointment books – in short, the busyness and officiousness of all these book-keepers, patent attorneys and lottery-ticket sellers with their triple-locked brief-cases like embassy attachés, when all they are carrying about are three dried out cheese sandwiches.

What is most typical of Berlin is deception: functional form, without solidity in either materials or execution; mechanics' apprentices who are above mere careful workmanship, and at once declare themselves fully fledged inventors or builders: streamlined kiddie cars with brittle imitation leather, 'functionally' constructed flashlights with inoperative connections, and the 'New Functionalism' which would make desks and beds out of reinforced concrete, and is really infinitely less practical than the so-called 'romantic' excesses of the past. And a few other items:

'Economy In Construction' and the junk called 'unfinished goods'; the ersatz-wool suit which is not warm and cannot be cleaned; and that snake poison made of sulphur and sugar and treated by all the hellish arts of I.G. Farben, which is sold by the glass as wine in the restaurants of the Westend: wine – this brew that is supposed to look and smell like the real thing, to have both body and flavour while costing next to nothing, which provides the unwary on the morning after with the legacy of a truly monstrous hangover.

No, I do not believe that there are many cities in which as much time is lost in useless bureaucratic reorganisation, rejoinders of 'On the other hand ...', purposeless chatter, and directorial pontification as in Berlin.

'When I am called to Babelsberg to show my rough script,' a film writer, a man of repute and titanic energy, told me recently, 'I find gathered around a large green table seven elderly gentlemen who obviously all have high blood pressure and who all have boxes of pills handy on the table before them. These gentlemen are all enchanted with my script. Then, just as everything appears settled, out of the shadows springs a dramatist's apprentice in horn-rimmed glasses. This is a type perfectly aware of his own superfluity, and so expends vast efforts in an attempt to find something wrong, and thus provide at least the shadow of a justification for his paltry 300 marks a month.

'This gentleman rises to say that the script is certainly wonderful, but that such and such scenes might give offence to the pressure group organised by the German wallpaper manufacturers, and that such and such other place in the script would not be comprehensible to inhabitants of Mars, prospective civil servants, or stenographers who had not graduated from high school. The reply that whatever purports to cover every contingency actually covers none, has no effect. The signal has been given for the elderly gentlemen to awaken from their lethargy long enough to attempt to legitimise their own, much higher, salaries. Each now racks his brain to add his own "now, on the other hand …" to the discussion. And so begins the nerve-racking period of weeks of smoke-filled story conferences, telephone calls, breakfasts, and still more story conferences which is known to every author working at the Babelsberg studios, and which ends finally in the complete junking of the original script. The new version has carefully eliminated every natural association in favour of a super-clever artificiality. In accord with the principle "Why have things simple when they can just as easily be complicated", an attempt is made to fly to the moon.

'Finally, all concerned are ready for a sanatorium, and the monstrous structure compounded of impotent intellectuality collapses of its own impossibility. There is a pause for a deep breath, and then the "simple, sound, completely satisfying solution" is found – in every detail, the same as in the original script.

'This fact is admitted amidst many apologies, tendered with hearty slaps on the back, and perhaps a certain faint embarrassment. The unfortunate part of it is that in the meantime the original impetus has been lost, and that four weeks of the three months assigned to making the film have been lost in useless discussion – weeks that must now be made up with frantic, hasty work.'

Isn't this Berlin? Isn't this the principle which has underlain all that has happened in this deeply hopeless city for the last sixty years ... industry, the arts, and not least, statesmanship, as well?

A General Staffer told me recently about an experience of his during the hot summer of 1917 on the Balkan front. 'It was July,' he told me, 'and we were under heavy pressure, so much so that sometimes we were no longer sure how we stood, when during a few minutes' time out for breakfast I was called to the telephone: the Chief himself. I recognised Ludendorff's voice, and despite the distance I could hear quite clearly. Astonishing to hear the question over the receiver, coming from beyond the Vosges Mountains, the Danube, the Rhine, and down the slopes of the mountains of the Balkans, repeated over and over: "Are there strawberries there?"

'I truly did not know what our lord and master was referring to. Was he, I wondered, enquiring after the menus of our frugal breakfasts, or could it be that he was no longer *all there*. Finally, after a period of painful confusion I grasped what he was after.

'He had heard that the land surrounding our occupied positions was eminently suited to raising strawberries. Concerned as he was with the state of the German economy, and at the same time with providing suitable employment for German soldiers who might at the moment be idle, he had conceived the idea of having us plant strawberries, proceeds from the sale of which should then go to bolster foreign exchange balances. It did no good at all for me to protest that we were being heavily pressed by the enemy and needed every available man – he had to have his strawberries.

'And he got them, too. We had to withdraw troops urgently needed at the front to do the planting. We did it with great misgivings, and had vast trouble afterwards to close the gaps so created. He actually got his strawberry acreage and the next year a bountiful yield, which he intended to have preserved in Berlin and sold abroad. The crop was really first-rate, but when it got to Berlin it was completely rotten, fermented, and mouldy. It had been shipped on the overtaxed railroads under heavy freight loads. All of it had to be thrown away.'

Thus my informant. Today, I dined at the little Italian restaurant on Anhalter Street, where I saw four higher-ranking SA officers, all thoroughly drunk, who kept yelling into the ears of the owner, who looked like a character in a Verdi opera, and at his Neapolitan waiters. The word they continually roared, on account of the newly concluded German-Italian friendship pact, was 'Collaborazione' … probably the only Italian word they knew. At the same time, behind me, another little scene, hardly less rich acoustically than the first, was being enacted. In this one, two ladies of the Berlin bourgeoisie, of the type described earlier, were deep in conflict over an evening coat which had fallen from the back of a chair to the floor. While the little Neapolitans watched, grinning, one of these ladies accused the other of deliberately throwing the garment down. At this, the second screeched: 'I beg your pardon, madam! I am a *German* woman!'

And thus it goes in Berlin.

At this moment, exhausted by the endless turning and clamour of this mill grinding on emptiness, I am back in my room in a hotel close to the Anhalter station. The place is furnished with the mass-produced junk of the years just before the war, and has walls that appear to be as thick as my finger. If I, here in my cell baked by the summer heat on the fourth floor, were for some reason to utter the word 'No!' even slightly louder than usual, I am certain that from the depths of the ground floor an oily baritone would respond in Balkan accents: 'Ah, perhaps you will think it over.'

And so it goes in the city of Berlin. This is a place of formulas and stereotypes. The only things that bloom here have to do with numbers, columns, formulas, and patterns. And with it all, there is this repulsive poverty, which has nothing to do with simplicity, which is merely a cover for inferiority and stupidity. Sparse and skimpy is the motto of this land. When I was still in short pants, I read that Frederick the Great's grenadiers wore waistcoats that were not waistcoats at all but merely triangles of red cloth which had been sewn to their doublets. And whether this story is true or not, I see these triangular pieces of cloth everywhere, in big things and small. Appearance, artifice, a patched-on thing, and with it all the deeply ingrained idea of being something special. Why? Because they have the urge to rob and pillage – which is characteristic of all who live meanly.

'Germany is never satiated; with no sense of form or taste, lacking all idea of what comforts and pleases in life, it has just one ambition: for more. And when it finally has more than it can possibly use, it puts what is left to one side, and woe to him who touches it! A nation of pirates, making its forays on dry land, but always with *Te Deums*, for the greater glory of God or the Faith. For there has never been a shortage of inscriptions to put on its flags in this land.'

Is this a Rhine Confederation intellectual speaking? Is this Bavarianism in the style of Doctor Sigl? No, this is Theodor Fontane, claimed by this city as one of its very own, a Prussian *pur sang*, as they say. I can cite myself here. I, too, am of old Prussian stock, although my mother was of Austrian descent.

I think back. My grandfather ('Who can be what his father was?' Hamsun says) ... my grandfather was a reserved and cultured man who lived the contemplative life, read Christian Garve and Humboldt, and retired at fifty to spend his remaining years hunting and fishing in *otium cum dignitate*. He represented the last of the genuine conservatives, the true Junkers – wonderfully cultivated, widely travelled, and sceptical of all bombast – whether out of the mouths of Hohenzollerns, or, as the East Prussians derisively called them, 'Nurembergians'.

It was the generation of the Franco–Prussian War, returning bloated with success from that militarily most wonderful but in its effects most unfortunate of all German wars, that broke the form. By a series of rich marriages, they allied themselves with industry and finance, and so opened the way for both to influence the government on a scale never known before. Let no one counter that the same thing happened in England during the early Victorian period, and in France during the Restoration. The medicine was absorbed by England without ill effect; it was harmful for France; and it proved to be a deadly poison for this country, which can and must base itself on agriculture and a pastoral economy. In 1853, Bismarck, standing at the graves of the dead of 1848, 'could not even forgive the dead'. Yet, eighteen years later, in the Hall of Mirrors at Versailles, he helped make the National Liberalism of these same dead the dominant ideology of Germany. Thus by his drive for industrial prosperity he undermined the foundations of the very state he had created.

Bülow, whose coarse-grained memoirs I read recently, described the effects of Bismarck's policy with '*Nul tissérand ne sait ce qu'il tisse*' ... a quotation which of course throws a great deal of light on the tragedy of a Reich formed without regard to geography. The 'form' (to use a Spenglerian concept) of this nation required that it avoid the expedients of industrial expansionism and capital investment. Everything that has befallen us since derives from the time when the Prussian oligarchy took industrial capital for its concubine. This is responsible for the breakdown of all the basic societal ties so necessary to a healthy Germany, and for making this a politically amorphous nation.

Beginning with that time, a geopolitically based policy for Germany was tossed overboard, and foreign policy was increasingly geared to the export market. Result: the First World War, waged completely 'against geography'.... Even before this, there was the unmitigated cynicism with which, around 1840, a generation brought up in the atmosphere of the student clubs and 'Turnvater Jahn' threw overboard its entire spiritual heritage ... the unbridled indulgence in dreams of a special, Teutonically embroidered prosperity, a shallow and irresponsible concentration on *one* generation, an unheard-of destruction of irreplaceable natural resources, of our cultural and ethical substance – a stockbroker's philosophy, already apparent in the sixties and seventies, which blocked out every thought about tomorrow....

Thus the Wilhelms led our society into the disastrously shapeless kind of thing in which men of learning became racing-drivers, bankers went in for breeding thoroughbreds, and cavalry lieutenants became absorbed in their industrial stocks ... and so lost themselves in the mob, became as faceless as the rest under the spell of the only banner that could have held this amalgam together: materialism ... and thus sank into a godforsaken troglodytism, which I believe has presaged certain destruction for a civilisation since the days of Caracalla. The ideal of the classless society as preached by Hitler is postulated on the limbless organism. But I believe that Nature, which in its very beginnings was *form* itself, abhors nothing as much as the amorphous.

I am writing this in a Berlin hotel which is about as quiet and discreet as a howitzer. At this moment, a lady on the floor below whose name probably is Dolinski and who is certainly of the type I described earlier, is giving all the details of her divorce to her friend at the other end of the telephone. The windows are open, and all the spicy details are as though implanted in the still, hot air. Finally, whether I want to or not I learn what drove Herr Dolinski prematurely out of Madame's arms. I hear it, and recall a parade of the League of German Maidens which I saw go past in the city yesterday ... a procession of bowlegs and broad hips marching between the ecstatically ugly façades of a city in love with its own ugliness, an exhibition of joylessness, a declaration of war on everything that 'comforts and pleases in life'.

Pondering the great changes of the nineteenth century, and with this procession of females still in my mind, I realise that the moment, seventy years ago, Germany in its infatuation with prosperity agreed to let Prussia be its organiser and procurer, it did not merely go to the dogs – much worse, it went to the *Dolinskis,* who inhabit this place, as well. Prussia is a state patched together out of bits and pieces. It was never intended to be a nation. To hold together the monstrous structure formed this way, the Prussians had to put all their energies into their military machine ... as a result, no middle class, no patrician class, and no true caste of the learned could ever come into being, and therefore, immediately following the disappearance of that oligarchy of mixed Vandal-Kashube antecedents described by Fontane, there rose to the surface that thoroughly un-German, that thoroughly colonial type which, when the men of the Holy Roman Empire were building cathedrals, was still busy tattooing green lizards around its belly button. The Elbe is a furrow in the landscape deeply significant in German history, and there are good reasons why certain species of birds and plants have never crossed from the left to the right bank of this river. For here, between the Elbe and the Vistula, is to be found the home of the Madonnas with the bowlegs previously mentioned; here, the breeding ground of this race with its eternal cry for *more*, the reservoir of all mass-man's repressed drives, the hatchery for all treaty breaches and the robberies masquerading as acts of state which Herr Hitler has committed these last five years – with no one daring to contradict him when he gave these as proof of his statesmanship.

Here, then, is where the preference for the provisional and second-rate was born. This disposition toward false-front ersatz can be seen even in the baroque trappings of the kings of Prussia, the gilded plaster of their palaces, accompanied by the demand, backed up by a gun, to please, if you will, be so kind as to accept all this as solid and definitive and fully valid. This, then, is where the eternal 'More! More!' originated, and the deification of the threadbare, the cult of the ugly, the gigantic fetishism which placed the statue of an 'iron-will Hindenburg' so that it towered over the trees of the Königsplatz; this is the place where the eye-bulging hatred against everybody who had more originated, the ceaseless eyeing of other people's property, the readiness to sudden banditry, and the drive to make this Prussian cult-of-the-threadbare into the state religion of Germany, and following that, of the entire world. And they will, if the other peoples prove recalcitrant, use their guns!

I recall the story of the corporal who told his infantrymen at the entrance to the church not to lose valuable time in 'sitting around, dozing' but to hurry and get done ('From the altar to the organ and from the priest out the door!') so as to use the time to better advantage elsewhere. This kind of thing was tolerable as long as a great and completely Machiavellian king used the army *'pour l'honneur de l'épée.'* But armed might in the service of I.G. Farben – the waging of war for the propagation of economy-in-construction, rayon stockings, and the ersatz suit – is to become the scourge and plague of the world, the *odium generis humani*, in a world of abundance and plenty. Germany turned ugly, and malignant, and the centre of the disasters that have been coming now at twenty-five-year intervals, the day Bismarck established a Reich, and a nation began to be ruled by a colony – Prussia.

And here I touch on the central political problem affecting Europe today. After the Prussian oligarchy – which was, at the very least, aware that it had responsibilities – disappeared, the men of Versailles were guilty of the incredible stupidity of dismembering Austria. After that, all that was needed was for Prussian greed to combine with a political condottiere – and the catastrophe which all of us knew was in the making was upon us.

In southern Germany, the bitter battle being fought below the surface against the Nazis is at the same time a battle against Prussianisation, and a defence of Germany's natural structure. This may be a German problem today, but tomorrow it will be a matter for Europe and the world to resolve. The time is fast approaching when Europe will have to decide whether it will let itself be engulfed by the gray wave, or finally defend its own heart from the drive for power of Prussianism.

9 September 1937

Most likely on the basis of a denunciation, the Gestapo appeared suddenly at the home of Theodor Häcker,[26] the theologian, who is keeping a journal, and made a search for the manuscript. One man actually picked up the document and was just about to read it when someone asked him a question, and the Gestapo man was distracted and put the manuscript down unread. Meanwhile, how poor Häcker – whose nerves are not too strong, anyway – must have trembled for his head as the seconds and minutes passed!

My friends have taken the occasion to give me warning about my own writings. Driven as I am by my own inner necessity, I must ignore the warning and continue these notes, which are intended as a contribution to the cultural history of the Nazi period. Night after night, I hide this record deep in the woods on my land ... constantly on watch lest I am observed, constantly changing my hiding place.

And this is how we now live, my vanished friends. Do you, who left Germany four and more years ago, have any idea of how completely without legal status we are, of what it is to be threatened with denunciation at any time by the next hysteric who comes along?

Strange to think of you, strange now to hear your voices through the ether and over the ocean depths, coming from a world so long since barred to us! Strange to happen into places where just a few years ago we used to talk. I miss you, miss you even though, as was true for most of you, you were opponents of mine and politically on the other side – oh, believe me, finally it is the lack of all opposition and any dissension whatsoever, and the deadly monotony that results, that makes life here so unbearable.

And yet, you will at first no longer understand us, who were your friends, when you come back to take up again the threads of our former ties. Or will you actually be able to understand that flight into civilisation was more comfortable than remaining at the dangerous outpost, an illegal watcher among the barbarians? Will you be able to grasp what it has meant to spend these long years with heart filled with hate, hate at lying down, and hate at rising, hate through the long hours of bad dreams – and all of this without rights under the law, without the smallest compromise, without a single 'Heil Hitler', a single attendance at a meeting – while through it all the stigma of illegality sits upon one's brow? Will we still speak the same language when this is over? Will you, surrounded as you have been all these years by all the appurtenances of civilisation ... grasp that the deathlike loneliness of our lives and the misery-laden air of the catacombs we have been breathing for so long have made our eyes terribly clear-sighted? May it not be, in the first moments after your return, that the visions these eyes can now see in the distance will frighten you?

What about the world of ideas of 1789 – the world which surrounds you, and which is still the basis for your lives and thought, as self-evident to you as the fact that a crab has its protecting shell? Understand me: we, here, know full well that all of this – encyclopaedism, the whole process begun with the Renaissance of divesting man of his gods – was once a vital way of life. Let no one do me the injustice of holding my visions to be the nightmares of a *homo temporis acti*, or the hallucinations of one feverish with the plague that surrounds him! But isn't what we are enduring here simply the final consequence of 1789? Hasn't the bourgeoisie, which in 1790 began to conceal its seizure of the heritage of power left by the kings with a cry of '*vive la nation*', shown itself to be a most unstable phenomenon? Didn't Balzac foretell the Russian, as well as the German, tragedy when he said that 'there will come a day when the bourgeoisie will hear its *Marriage of Figaro* played?' Didn't St Just so long ago announce the coming of this insane totalitarianism of the state? And doesn't Girondism reach its final flower in the Krupps, the Vögelers, Röchlings and Associates, as cynically, throwing aside every restraint, they make themselves the centre of all things German, the focal point of German society – militant Girondism, devoid of all basic ethical content, sworn enemy of men of faith, ideological victor of Waterloo even though defeated on the battlefield?

As far as National Socialism is concerned, I am sure that there will be agreement in seeing in it the arch-destroyer of a nation which has always tended towards the magical and unknown, and none of you, my old friends, will argue with me when I say that in 1500 there was a German nation, but no nationalism, whereas today, when our eyes are supposed to light up at every trouser button 'Made in Germany', we have the reverse: nationalism, and no nation. We will certainly be in agreement that this plutocratic government with its Hitler placed in the saddle by Herr Thyssen[27] and his friends reveals itself, in its complete demoralisation of the masses, to be nothing more than one last desperate attempt to prolong the nineteenth century....

Oh, no, there will be no lack of agreement when we again meet on a total rejection of the German present! But will we still be in agreement when we come to talk about the future? You will have just returned from a civilisation which is securely based for the present; will you still understand, or will you turn violently away from us when we tell you what we now see:

The Hitlerism is only a symptom, indicating a deep disturbance of cosmic proportions in the world; that we have now come to the end of five centuries of rationalism and free thought; that in the area occupied by mankind, a new factor, the irrational, has again made its appearance.

Shall we, whose eyes have been opened by our long martyrdom, overlook the signs of world crisis ... the writing on the wall in the palaces of human rationality you thought were so indestructible? Is it really an accident that precisely in the exact sciences the bases are shaking? That the laws of gravity are now said to be 'macro-physically' correct, only? That by the latest measurements of the speed of light, astrophysics has suddenly transferred the earth, that tiny ball of yesterday, into the centre of a circumscribed cosmos? And that, scenting the bankruptcy of the last five centuries, the philosophers have come up with a shabby 'as if' theory to prop up what little has been left standing amid the ruins?

I believe that mankind's great spiritual evolutions basically affect physical life on earth, and that if the demoralisation of its inhabitants continues, the planet will be destroyed by its own non-viability, and crack into pieces in some kind of cosmic catastrophe. But what I see coming is not basically a cosmic, but a historical phenomenon: the inevitable catastrophic finale to mass-thought, and thus to mass-man, which is in the making here and which now I see on the horizon in all its frightfulness and all its promise.

What else can the meaning be of this pervasive feeling of total bankruptcy, this secret fear and trembling like the feeling which precedes a great storm, of these spiritually empty people? We live in a gigantic spiritual vacuum. At any moment, awareness of the vacuum, and of horrifying chaos, could bring cataclysm. Mass-man, by mental and physical necessity, can only exist in his self-made womb of corruption and troglodytism. This is as neces-sary to him as mud to a pig. But what will he do if tomorrow his slimy cocoon is swept away?

I do not doubt that the contemporaries of Caracalla lived in a similar spiritual eclipse. I am well aware how badly these poor lines fall short of bearing true witness to this deepest degradation into which man has ever fallen. Recently, following the rain of Nazi bombs on unhappy Spain, I read again Rilke and Stefan George ... and laid them down again in the knowledge that all that I once had loved has become faded and mouldy in the air we have been breathing for years now, and that though Rilke is honest and deeply moving, his is only a tired game with dead forms; while George, in the red glare of a world on fire, is revealed as a pretentious poseur.

Doesn't the artist who claims that he can compose a string quartet now, or build a cathedral that can be something more than a blasphemy in stone, stand revealed before us as a liar and a fraud? As artists, are we not all standing before a wall, awaiting the appearance of the invisible hand striking against the wall – until the hand *does* appear? And what are the words, 'The end of the world is at hand', which Dostoyevsky wrote in his journal seventy years ago, but a presentiment of the apocalyptic horsemen now thundering down upon us, and a prophecy of how utterly lost we have become?

No, I am not a millenarian, and a passionate belief in life's regenerative powers makes me believe that the catastrophe I foretell will only be one more of many this planet has already seen. Nevertheless, I have come to the conclusion that the somatisation of life, which has been going on since the Renaissance, and which has been made complete these last years, has increasingly destroyed the balance between body and mind – and that without this balance physical life on the earth is impossible.

Doctors who attended the athletes at the Olympics of hallowed memory last year told me that menstrual disturbances in the girls and sexual insufficiency among the men of apparently boundless vigour of this extremely sports-minded generation were almost something like the rule (and not merely among the 'champions' but among the average participants). There could be no better proof that the somatisation of life destroys life itself. Gasoline, as the basis for all motorised happiness, has contributed more to the inner decay of mankind than alcohol.

And as regards mass-man – to be found in the uniform of a general or in the form of a university professor more often, almost, than in the overalls of a lathe-operator; mass-man who in his explosive reproductiveness, his corruption of all organic growth, and his biological instability finds a parallel only in the entirely similar cancer cell – his life cycle has already been completed once on this globe. Within two hundred years, bustling Rome had shrunk to the size of a provincial town, and the hermae and monumental structures of the Forum were half lost in fields of wheat.

The technology and mechanisation so essential to the biological existence of mass-man may not be affected by the kind of reversal in mode of life which we know happened in the agony of the ancients. But the sediment of stenographers now spreading over the earth ... the conglomeration of superfluous bureaucrats sending out totally useless questionnaires to paralyse areas which are still productive – they will not escape, if only because the rise of 'national' industries in former markets will make it impossible for Europe to go on exporting its surpluses; and it will become impossible to sustain rabbit-like reproduction.

But truly I do not see how, after the breakdown of all known forms, and the emergence of a new conception – which I foresee – technology and mechanisation can escape being relegated to the dust heap, or at least to the periphery of life. Only the 'New Adam', a savage who by an accident still has a white skin; who today uses all this equipment with an unconcern bordering on impudence; to whom it never occurs that one must replenish the thought-world from which all this technology derives; only mass-man can doubt its destructibility. If only to maintain his own existence, this anonymous mass thing takes refuge in a world into which no question of the possible insufficiency of this can possibly enter. Any number of once great civilisations may lie in ruins about mass-man: in his world, the four-cylinder engine is a piece of eternity. In this atmosphere, filled with sweaty faith in progress, man's knowledge has been steadily widened from the nature-philosophers of antiquity up to and including the most up-to-date college instructor. And if we can all just manage to live long enough, we will reach the point – thanks to this uninterrupted progress of mankind – when another college instructor drags His last heavenly secret out of God.

Ortega y Gasset sees in the dull matter-of-factness with which the 'up-and-coming young man of today' takes for granted the existence of the radio and the electric engine a clear indication of detachment from reality. He rightly quotes Weyl, the scientist, according to whom 'the apathy of a single generation would suffice to destroy the intellectual climate essential for the survival of technology.'

Is it possible to ignore any longer the fact that all of this is part of a terminal stage of a great culture, and that, its vigorous days long since over, technology itself is threatened by the intellectual impotence of mass-man?

Mass-man, who buys the products of technology in complete mindlessness, without involving himself, or even taking an interest in the intellectual work that made these things possible – mass-man is blood brother in this to the Roman of Caracalla's time, who was aware of the *Limes romanus* as a comforting guarantee for his comfortable way of life – but unable to rouse himself from his indolence to keep it from falling to pieces.

I do not believe that this 'New Adam' has the faintest idea of how completely dependent his existence is on the products of technology. I have an idea that at the beginning of the end of the world he will want to know how the government proposes to hold next Sunday's Germany–Sweden football match on schedule. His fate appears to me certain and unavoidable. The coming Second World War will be the beginning of the end: the end of an epoch in which rationalism was dominant, and the legacy of which – assuming that the planet is still capable of regeneration – will be 'X', a new mode of life based on the nonrational.

This being so, and the masses sensing that they are doomed, they will, no doubt, strike out against everything that is not mass-like, but is, simply, 'different'. In Germany, whose Hitler regime is simply a massive attempt to prolong the existence of mass-man, the target will be that small elite which has done more harm to this regime with its principled 'No' than all the Chamberlain policy of impotence and endless appeasement. I believe that our martyrdom, the fate reserved for our little phalanx, is the price for a rebirth of the spirit, and that realising this, we can hope for no more good during what remains of our ruined and brutalised lives on earth than that there may be meaning to the manner of our deaths.

I, who set this down, know myself to be in no way above the general fear of dying, and I know, too, that all large statements sooner or later come back to the man who makes them, and require redemption....

But we cannot go back to the life we shared with you yesterday, a life which you will spread before us so temptingly when you return. We have suffered too much to believe any more that the way to what we see as the Absolute can go in any other direction than through the deep valley of sorrow. Hell has not opened before our eyes to no purpose, and he who has once seen it cannot find his way back to earthly symposiums. Earlier, I recounted how a Hitler Youth threw the image of the Saviour into the street yelling, 'Lie there, you dirty Jew!' I have told about Hitler himself, and how he showed himself before the mob assembled at Berchtesgaden, and how afterward bewitched females swallowed the gravel his feet had trodden ... oh, it is the most shameful thing of all that this was not even the physically beautiful and spiritually glittering antichrist of the legends, but only a poor dung-face, in every aspect something akin to a *middle-class antichrist....*

Oh, truly, men can sink no lower. This mob, to which I am connected by a common nationality, is not only unaware of its own degradation but is ready at any moment to demand of every one of its fellow human beings the same mob roar, the same gravel-swallowing, the same degree of degradation.

When I got home, I turned to Dostoyevsky, to him who is proscribed in Germany as no one else. I read once more in *The Possessed* the words spoken by Peter Stepanovich, the son of the General's wife:

All are slaves and equal in their slavery. Everyone belongs to all, and all to everyone, and the great thing about it is equality. To begin with, the level of education, and science, and talents is lowered. A high level of education and science is only possible for great intellects, and they are not wanted. The great intellects have always seized power and been the despots. Great intellects cannot help being despots, and they've always done more harm than good. They will be banished or put to death. Cicero will have his tongue cut out, Copernicus will have his eyes put out, Shakespeare will be stoned. Down with culture. We've had enough of scholarship. Discipline comes first. The one thing wanting in the world is discipline. The drive for knowledge is an aristocratic drive we will destroy; we'll employ drunkenness, slander, spying; we'll stifle every genius in its infancy. We'll reduce all to a common denominator! Complete equality, absolute submission, absolute loss of individuality, the Pope at the head, with us 'round him, and below us – Shigalovism! ... But one or two generations of vice are essential now; monstrous, abject vice by which a man is transformed into a loathsome, cruel, egoistic reptile. There's going to be such an upset as the world has never seen before. Russia will be overwhelmed with darkness, the earth will weep for its old gods....

Truly, Dostoyevsky is right, the end of the world is at hand. It is the end, even if it is the end of *one* world, the tear-drenched and curse-ridden world of yesterday.

9 September 1937

I have spent several days at Hohenschwangau Castle as a guest of our Royal Master.[28] Released by my host following long talks lasting far into the night, I tried to get to my room in a distant guest wing, and, wandering through a maze of corridors up and down stairways unable to find the light switches in the unfamiliar surroundings, ended by crouching on a step and so waited, chattering with cold, for dawn.

My host related all kinds of stories to me, tales which in these times seemed to come to me from across an immense distance: about the triple-pronged cigar holder intended to hold three Havanas which he had seen Bismarck using – only by smoking three cigars at one time could that outsized glutton get the clouds of smoke he wanted; and about the marvellous appetite of the old Kaiser, with whom, shortly before the fateful year of 1888, he had breakfasted. Finally, he told me also of the gloomy and difficult days he had known as an army commander in the World War shortly before the collapse ... at that time, September 1918, the whole Army reserve had shrunk to half a company, and the airmen with the Army group had a gasoline stockpile of not quite 1,200 litres at their disposal.

At the end, my host showed me a photo in the *Berliner Illustrierte Zeitung* of Herr Göring, that happy family man, pictured in his study with his lady, the former Miss Sonnemann. They stood before an immense Gobelin tapestry which had been part of the Wittelsbach private collection, and which had *brevi manu* been stolen just as, probably, were the other items in this representative photograph: the enormous rings on the fingers of the master of the house and the bracelets and earrings on his wife. We spoke of the origins of this dainty fellow, the son of a Rosenheim waitress, who had not succeeded in gaining admission to a Bavarian cadet corps – the application had gone through the hands of the Crown Prince – and had thereupon been sent off to Prussia. Now, of course, along with a fantastic coat of arms, Herr Göring has had a pedigree drawn up which traces his descent to some Westphalian general of the early Middle Ages. Obviously mentally deranged, he now takes himself to be the King of Prussia in person. An acquaintance of mine, who had occasion to go to Karinhall recently, saw porcelain nameplates on the doors of the rooms occupied by the divers companions of the former Miss Sonnemann which read 'First Lady-in-waiting', 'Second Lady-in-waiting', etc.

But this is how they all are with one another, just this way. All of them act the *classa dirigente*, have fantastic coats of arms drawn up, compose even more fantastic pedigrees for themselves, and choose their 'adjutants' from among these north German nobility come down in the world who crowd after them just as the type that once followed Bockelson.

Herr Göring officially decrees that his wife is to be addressed as 'Your Ladyship', Herr Goebbels has some mangy princeling from a Middle German royal family, to pay him homage, and even Herr Himmler, who generally has taken pains to maintain a simple standard of living, is supposed to have a royal vassal in his entourage. But worst of all are the females, these former barmaids, most of whom have passed through any number of hands, who are loaded down with the stolen jewels of noble families, and still can never dispel the aura of their native kitchen milieu. Made up to resemble something midway between a movie star and a cocotte, they play at court intrigue: 'How, Frau Goebbels, does it happen that I observe three official cars constantly at the disposal of your husband, when he is actually entitled only to two?'

But this is the way they all are. The pose of revolutionaries, *de facto* dirty little bourgeoisie who cannot rid themselves of the feel of the dog collars they wore only yesterday, and who – the candles burned low and the food partly eaten – have seated themselves at the table of their evicted lords.

On the way home, I heard the latest scandal. The first year after they came to power, the Nazis proclaimed that duelling belonged to the natural rights of every man – a consistent extension of the philosophy of 1789 – and with much fanfare announced that all classes of society now had state approval for this method of solving differences. Any difference of opinion between master and servant over badly polished shoes could be resolved with pistols. But the very first duel held under the new dispensation has struck down one of their own – and by an ancient law, not the worst of the lot. Herr Roland Strunck, a journalist of a calibre that exceeded their usual level of the schoolmaster gone berserk – as far as I know, a decent chap, a man of some quality.

Strunck, then, discovered one day that a fellow Party member, a young lout, was carrying out Nazi tenets on sexual unrestraint by sleeping with Strunck's daughter. He called the fellow out and was killed. The duelling regulation has now been rescinded.[29] Now, a mere challenge has been made punishable by a heavy prison sentence, and the danger that a man may have to receive his chauffeur's seconds because he complained of his badly washed car has been set aside.

I had a disagreement about this policy with Clemens von Franckenstein, whom much travelling about has made into a sceptic. I have just finished *Action for Slander*, a novel in which two English cavalry officers seek satisfaction over an argument at baccarat first by boxing, and then by taking the matter to court – without the officers being suspended, and without the writer, Mary Borden, being able to give her bemused non-English readers so much as an inkling of what her two main characters might be like.

Now, I am far from being an advocate of the well-known idiotic student bloodletting, but I cannot possibly ignore the fact that since 1918, and the official ban on duelling, there has come about a complete bolshevisation of all standards of honour, and that a man's good name has become free game. Any libeller does not now have to fear the serious consequences that would have followed in the past – and this did not begin with the Nazis. Let no one, please, answer me with the ancient objection that generally the lie emerges for what it is. To take a libeller to court is really giving a small devil more than his due – besides which, when a defamation case involves family honour and the most private matters, a duel becomes an infinitely more human expedient than exposing the entire inner workings of one's home and life to newspaper stories, and oneself to running the gauntlet of the clacking tongues in the streets. We have witnessed an appalling decline in European mores these last thirty years. We shall have to take care not to sink even lower.

On the way home, I went through Munich, a city which I avoid as much as possible since its occupation by the Prussians – it was so gay and so brilliant, once! Not long ago the periphery of the city was untouched meadowland, stretches of bucolic peacefulness unlike anything else in Germany. This has been ruined by the depositing of hills of gravel, by the cutting down of the forests, by railroad spurs, and by monstrous industrial plants which the General Staff, with characteristic barbarian inability to understand that some things are irreplaceable, had finally brought here too. No, I no longer recognise Munich as the gay, high-spirited city of youth and happiness that it once was; never actually a big city, it was really only the main town of a land of peasants and farmers. Now, wide-hipped females, wives of the Prussian bureaucrats who are overrunning Bavaria, push their baby carriages past the façade of the Florentine Palace on Ludwigstrasse, and everywhere in the hotel corridors one sees in front of doors the repulsive jackboots of the newly promoted officers with their sergeant's faces. The

Friedrich Percyval Reck-Malleczewen (1925).

Irmgard Reck-Malleczewen, Reck's second
wife, with his poodle Klaus (1936).

Reck at Schleißheim, the large rambling estate
near Munich that he was forced to sell (1928).

A photograph taken in 1935 when Reck, a keen mountaineer, climbed the Alps.

After selling off Schleißheim, Reck bought a disused monastery in Poing (also near Munich) 50 miles from the Austrian border. Seen here with Klaus, his poodle (1930).

Back to back with his wife Irmgard at their new home in Poing.

In front of the main house of the monastery (1935).

In Poing on the bank of the river Alz (1936).

Distracted, at the entrance of Poing
under the woodcarving of St George
slaying the dragon.

The overgrown arbour at Poing (1938).

Reck playing with the Märklin steam engine which powered his train set (1941).

Reck seated in the library, which was terrorised by his pet parrot (1943).

Hoftheater, which in the last three years, since Franckenstein's departure, has sunk, really, to the level of a fourth-rate touring company, is packed with herds of BDM (Bund Deutscher Mädchen – League of German Maidens) bleach-blondes, and the hotels are crowded with the wives of north German factory managers, the bane of every porter's existence, keeping their rendezvous with Nazi gangsters. No, I want to see nothing more of this city ruined by Prussian barbarism until the day of release.

While in the once secluded Hofgarten, where, incidentally, Herr Hitler wants to build 'the greatest opera house in the world' by having the arcades and Rottmann frescoes removed, the painter Ziegler was pointed out to me.[30] He has been assigned by Hitler to 'cleanse German art of all decadence' and is, therefore, something like the chief among all German painters: a man with no back to his head. He holds the title of 'Master of Female Pubic Hair', conferred on him by his associates in view of his predilection for this kind of representation.

And so it goes in Munich. The general feeling about the systematically pursued Prussianisation of the city has, moreover, been shown in an occurrence which in the days of the old Regents thirty years ago would have been dismissed as incredible. The outlying districts of Haidhausen and Giesing, Munich's lively and alley-filled versions of Whitechapel, have for some time been made unsafe by a group of adolescents banded together under the sign of the 'Red Anchor',[31] who have launched a campaign of terror against all wearing Nazi uniforms. Provided one does not break the taboo against speaking north German dialect here, he can with a quiet heart traverse Giesing wearing a fur coat and top hat, and he will not be troubled – the 'Red Anchor' lays hands only on uniformed Nazis, and especially members of the SS. All this is in no wise to be dismissed as harmless rowdyism, since the 'Red Anchor' is said to be responsible for a number of killings. The police have recovered the corpses of several SS members, and connected the murders with the honourable brotherhood. The comedy here is that the entire band has been recruited from young fellows, *de facto* anti-Nazis, who were forced into the Hitler Youth and are now playing double roles. But what verges on the incomprehensible is that in circumstances that approach those of the Chicago underworld, the leader of the organisation is supposed to be a Munich lawyer – this in our lighthearted basically goodhumoured city, over which just two and a half decades ago a dignified old patriarch held sway! Truly, a devil has broken loose from his leash in Germany – ah, and we none of us know how we are to get him back on the chain again.

20 March 1938

And now, Austria.

We have seen it coming for weeks. Naturally, we sensed what it all meant, these threats and staged riots … the whole shabby performance designed to provide an excuse for intervention. And now tank and artillery columns are rolling down every street, under the command of agitated young SS men, and in my village, exactly as though this were a battle of life and death, the half-grown louts in the Hitler Youth are playing at being heroes, and volunteering for the Army as though the enemy was a European Great Power, and not a tiny nation of seven million inhabitants.

I cannot help but see in this generalised brutality, this nasty satisfaction over the fate of the Austrian leaders, this general delight in ridicule and rape – something ignoble, which makes me deeply ashamed....

Austria, poor, eternally derided Austria, whose only sin was, that until the end, and in the face of the attack on it by Greater Prussia, it held to a last recollection of the noble old Holy Roman Empire of the Germans.

Now in Salzburg, where I have been staying these past few days, these Berlin potato-faces fill the streets, together with their full-bosomed females. Thanks to the rate of exchange they are able to make off with everything for a song, including goods which are no longer available in Germany, and the store shelves are empty. They are behaving like a horde of servants whose masters are away, who have found the keys to the wine cellars and now are having an orgy with their women....

> The gang are out of the house,
> Let us drink down all they've left,
> A kiss from you
> And a kiss from you,
> Life at last, life at last
> is what it should be.

Something of the sort. Swarms of Berlin League of German Maidens girls have been directed here for the moment, and they wave ecstatically at the tank columns rattling through the old streets. In the next issue of the *Berliner Illustrierte Zeitung* they will be pictured as 'Local Inhabitants, Who Greeted Their German Liberators with Wild Ovations'.... We know all about the talent for stagecraft of Goebbels, the limping haberdashery salesman.

I hear that Schuschnigg[32] is being held in the foulest kind of prison, and mishandled. They are all enjoying themselves over the misfortunes of people who had the temerity to stick to their posts to the end.

Since it would be quite inconceivable for the writers – their writers – to absent themselves from the universal bacchanalia, Herr Bruno Brehm has come forward with a secretly printed brochure to mark the event. This contains a hymn to Hitler, who is lauded by this traitor to his people as the consummator of the dream of a German Reich.

But the low point is reached when the north German press dares to speak of 'Austria's return to the Reich' – as though these Prussians had any rightful claim to be considered the successors of the great empire of the Hohenstaufens and Habsburgs.... As much right as a swineherd who rises in the world, marries the daughter of an ancient family fallen on evil days, and then claims he is in direct line of descent and entitled to bear the family shield.

I spoke to my cousin, L., who is participating as a major general in this political burglary and cannot conceive why my eyes are not bright with pure joy at the event. I asked him if he imagined that a man of breeding like the elder Moltke would not have reacted with an immediate resignation if he had been given orders to make an attack of this kind. The frightening and incredible thing is that these Prussian officers, bearers of great and famous names, have no conception of the degraded roles they have been led to play here. It is this erasure of a feeling of honour, this ethical defect, this Godless denial that boundaries exist between right and wrong that forces me to believe in a final and ignominious depth of the German spirit.

Deeply moving stories are told, of Austrian officers turning their guns against themselves, of units from Bregenz who placed themselves in position for a hopeless battle against the invader; of ordinary soldiers of the old Salzburg Rainer regiment, who threw themselves from the castle windows of the Salzburg fortress at the humiliation of their country. Why in the world did Schuschnigg not give the order to shoot, in one last attempt to awaken the rest of the world from its incomprehensible lethargy with these shots? The bordering countries watched this miserable rape of a little nation, and shrugged their shoulders. Nobody is moving to stop this before it is too late. It almost seems that they prefer to stand back and wait until the cobra breaks out.

But I foresee a day when the nations will regret their cowardly passivity. The cost is beyond measuring; but they will have to pay, someday. In this first great breach of the peace, the criminal has been let go unpunished and is thus made to appear more powerful than he is. And as he is made more powerful, we, who are his last opponents inside Germany, are made weaker and more impotent.

Are we, and all who think like us, to run into the machine guns of a Nazi army which, thanks to the lethargy of the governments, now has Austria's guns as well? I put the question now, and see the day coming when I will ask it a second time: after the inevitable Second World War. If five years ago, at the time of the so-called Assumption of Power, the European nations had taken action – everything would have ended with a police raid, with the gang being hustled off to jail by the collars.

But what did everyone do? They stood by and watched, and thus made impossible any resistance from inside Germany. What are they doing now? They are standing by and watching, preoccupied with figuring out a way to avoid irritating Herr Hitler – and so making any resistance even more impossible. In time to come, you will be able to do certain things: you will be able to punish those who with their wretched political deals made possible that infamous day in January 1933; and you will be able to punish the military and industrial men-behind-the-scenes. But one thing you will not be able to do: you will not be able to make the whole nation, in extenso, responsible for a regime which you – yes, you – have strengthened. You have broken our internal resistance through political lethargy, and you are nevertheless demanding of an unarmed people that they do what you, with your mighty armies and the most powerful navy in the world, do not dare.

There will come a day when you will come face to face with this reproach, and this accusation.

As I write, an immense flight of bombers is droning past overhead. For a whole hour the drone has gone on above, as though these planes were flying against a world power. I am a German, I encircle this land in which I live with all my love. Never again can I be torn from here without going to seed. I tremble for each tree and each wood that disappears, for each silent valley that is devastated, for each stream that these pirates of industry, the real masters of our land, threaten....

I know that this land is the living, beating heart of the world. I will go on believing in this heartbeat, despite all the covering layers of blood and dirt. But I know also that the thing up there that rumbles and thunders is the denial of right and justice, of truth and faith and everything that makes life worth living. I believe that this is a caricature of Germany, smeared by a malignant ape escaped from the leash.

You, up there: I hate you waking and sleeping. I will hate and curse you in the hour of my death. I will hate and curse you from my grave, and it will be your children and your children's children who will have to bear my curse. I have no other weapon against you but this curse, I know that it withers the heart of him who utters it, I do not know if I will survive your downfall.

But this I know, that a man must hate this Germany with all his heart if he really loves it. I would ten times rather die than see you triumph.

Writing this, I shrink inside myself. Soon it will be Easter, and as though in derision the final chorus of the *St Matthew Passion* rings out from the radio at just this moment – '*Wir setzen uns in Tränen nieder ...*'

Germany, my Germany ... yes, this chorus, once this spoke for us.

And now?

Now, still, overhead, these white savages steer their moronic automatons, flying toward brutality and crime, drowning out the peaceful stillness of this spring day. I am crying. But it is more out of fury and shame than out of sadness....

July 1938

Herr Schmeling has been beaten in New York.

By order of King Mob, I am supposed to believe in a defeat for all Germans because the highly paid German butcher boy who was knocked down in New York by another highly paid butcher boy happens to have the same nationality as I! Four of us sat until the dawn of this warm summer day to hear the outcome of this fight. When we heard that the entire drama over there had been played out in two minutes, we broke into laughter. My dear countrymen, I hope that you will live to see the day when you learn to believe in other gods than a few movie whores and a couple of prize-fighters.

One summer morning, I noticed three men surveying my fields. They were strangers, and their whole appearance was dissonant in this peaceful atmosphere. They were going about my fields and property with all kinds of measuring instruments, did not bother to greet me when they saw me, and then, when I questioned them, identified themselves as employees of the Berlin Siemenswerke. It seemed that Siemens, one of the biggest of Göring's enterprises, was planning to build a factory here....

Without querying me, without arrangement with me, without any notice, and without even an attempt to provide the shadow of legality. I asked how Siemens would like it if I appeared unheralded on their property and proceeded to drill holes. This led to a lively exchange, and since I wanted to acquaint the gentlemen from Berlin with basic concepts of propriety and good manners, I simply called my people and had the instruments removed from their possession and placed under lock and key.

This led to loud outcries and many threats. The next day the assistant regional commissioner arrived. After mildly reproaching me for my resort to force, he informed me that I could expect to receive the visit of a commission in two days. This commission appeared as scheduled: five Bavarian administrative officials and an Austrian engineer sporting a swastika on his lapel. I learned the essentials of this project, which calls for the devastation of the whole of this marvellous river valley, the demolition of my ancient, early Gothic house, and putting four hundred hectares under water.

All this to achieve 4,000 hp, the equivalent of the energy produced by one bomber. This by a regime which is constantly proclaiming its partiality to the farmers, and which has adopted as one of its many slogans, that 'Germany will either be a country of farmers, or it will be nothing.' From the first words spoken I understood that what was involved here had less to do with 4,000 horsepower than with a project that would allow north German industry to transfer its capital to the south. Smelling the approach of war and its accompanying inflation, these industrialists are converting their paper money into fixed assets – assets to be stolen from the farmers, no matter what the cost in natural resources, and loss of livelihood to the people involved. All this is given the name of the 'general good' to cover the brutal character of the actions of these industrial robber barons who are the successors of the German dynasties and the old nobility.

I thought of the stillness of this incomparable river valley, and of the eighteen generations of men to whom this land has given shelter and sustenance. I saw no reason to hide my indignation....

The Bavarian officials were quietly on my side, and their grins showed it. But the Austrian engineer was enraptured with Hitlerism and a heated exchange followed. He spoke of 'the good of society', and I asked him what the current market quotation was for this 'society'. When he began to talk about expropriation I declared that it was quite possible that I might have to leave this house, but that if I did he would certainly leave it beforehand – on a stretcher, and feet first.

Evidently people in Germany have become unaccustomed in recent years to hearing plain talk of this kind, and he was speechless with fury. Nevertheless, the possibility that I might have my revolver ready in my pocket made him shift in doubt and fear in his chair. As the Bavarians stared at me as if at some miraculous animal, he quickly amended that it was possible the whole matter might take years to resolve. And with this, the commission departed.

Some time later I learned in Munich something of the background of this. A source in the Hydroelectric Construction Section of the Ministry for the Interior told me that there had for a long time been extant another proposal, which would have obtained the same amount of power but would have spared the entire valley. But this proposal had been rejected, because Councillor Arno Fischer, chief of the section and inventor of the underwater turbine, wanted to use these turbines throughout the project. This, of course, would be of the greatest incidental benefit to this gentleman's pocket, and it was for the sake of these underwater turbines and the inventor's pocket that the entire valley was to be sacrificed. Lurking further in the background, a big Bavarian chemical company, which had long been producing explosives, and behind this again the all-powerful Herr Göring – Göring, who was making regular appearances in debtor's court only a couple of years ago and now has become lord and master over the fate of families of ancient peasant stock.

This was the reason, then. According to my confidant, there is no longer a property in Germany that is safe from this sort of thing. We will see, Messieurs, we will see. Ah, I would rather see my property and all of Germany blown to bits than leave it to such as these....

September 1938

Homeward-bound from Berlin, which I found nervous and already a little more constrained as the Czech crisis continues, I saw from my sleeper window in the Upper Palatinate endless trains loaded with artillery and munitions rolling towards the border. Germany, by which I mean this latest generation, carefully nurtured in the precepts of highway robbery, is indeed in a most unusual state of mind today. It regards the will of this so-called Führer as a kind of cosmic law, and all opponents, even those outside the Reich's borders, as criminals. Yes, of course, a foreign nation is involved, and there is the little matter of broken treaties but then the Führer has willed it so....

And what if the others were finally to take courage in hand and say 'No' to this Führer grown drunk on the success of his political burglaries? It could be that the shock of learning that he is not, as he has gradually come to believe, the centre of the world, would be enough. That moment when, for the first time, he does not get his way, he might well simply disappear from the stage.

But everything indicates that Europe will look on and do nothing, this time as in the attack on Austria. And so Hitler's position will be further strengthened. These are the lengths to which we have been driven: that we, who are not the worst of the Germans, must now put our hopes in a war to free us as of a plague of locusts.

I had a long discussion on the subject with P., who cannot comprehend why I feel this way. Of course, he is a businessman, and it has long been a theory of mine that the basic substance of nationalism is of a commercial nature. Besides, it depends on whether or not one recognises this regime, born in chicanery, blackmail, and swindle, as a legitimate government. I have, since 30 January 1933, never ceased to view it as criminal in nature, and as a fraudulent counterfeit of a modern state. If, then, a gang of thieves breaks into my house, and attacks and beats me, shall I then complain about the police who come to my rescue and break down the barricaded door?

I can now prove that the plebiscite to legitimise Hitler's take-over of Austria was falsified in the crudest possible way. Together with the other four adults of my house, I naturally voted 'No'. In addition, I know of at least twenty other reliable people in the town who did the same. Nevertheless, according to the official results, the town unanimously and without a single dissenting voice 'approved the actions of the Führer'.

The air is full of rumours about plots and assassinations centring, oddly enough, about the Praetorian Guard of the SS, and the so-called Knights of the Teutonic Order (mainly druggists' assistants and mail clerks). And this is what happened to me in Munich recently....

As I was shaving in the little hotel near the main station where I ordinarily stay, something dropped past my third-storey window, and then there was the sound of a heavy thud. When I left the hotel a man was lying in the street, legs spread wide, skull cracked, and brains in a pool of blood on the pavement. He wore black riding pants and a gray and white striped pyjama jacket.

Bystanders stood about, gawking, and an excited bicyclist was telling how he had been nearly hit by the body plummeting from the fourth floor. A noisy woman had actually seen the man climb onto the window ledge just before he jumped. A hotel porter covered the corpse with a heap of paper while two street cleaners swept up the blood and brains. Then came a sanitation truck, a hose was connected to the nearest hydrant, and the pavement was hosed clean as the corpse lay alongside, boots protruding beyond the covering paper.

The corpse remained in the now closed-off side street, its outspread legs coming into view whenever the wind lifted the brown hill of paper. When I questioned the porter, he told me that the man had appeared at the hotel that morning at six o'clock, in SS uniform and slightly drunk, and had asked for a room on the uppermost floor available. He then ordered a litre of beer and a whole bottle of cognac – the remains of which we then found, the cognac three-quarters gone, in the bare little attic room alongside the disordered bed. On the floor also lay the man's black jacket, and strewn on the bed, a crumpled collection of the kind of post-cards which are sold to the tourist on the Praça do Commercio in Lisbon, and above all in Port Said.

The results of the preliminary police investigation emerged several hours later. The dead man, who had registered, naturally, under a false name, had been trained in the school at Bad Tölz for SS officers. He had been involved in a conspiracy against Hitler and the Nazis, and was being hunted.

The incident in all its unpleasantness and its still more unpleasant corpse reminded me of a story that my friend Hans von Bülow, nephew of the great general, told me years ago. In 1918, during the Finnish campaign, a former Prussian officer was captured who had become the chieftain of a band of Bolsheviks. This man had spent years in a Russian prisoner-of-war camp, and this experience and his life during the Revolution had turned him entirely into a marauder. Before the war, the man had been promoted from the ranks, and from 1912 he had been given the privileges of an officer. Now this man, who had been completely brutalised by four years in a Siberian prison camp and had degenerated into a bearded, bloody killer, was condemned to death as the leader of a gang which had committed endless crimes. But this is what is so incredible: as he stood before the firing squad, looking into the black eyes of the muzzles directed on him, he asked for a cigarette. He lit the cigarette, took a puff or two, and then in the instant before the command was given to fire ripped down his pants, whirled about giving death his blank behind, dropped a pile on the ground, and received the sacrament and the bullets simultaneously – as he continued to defecate.

I talked to Bülow again about that old story. At first glance, there was a passing resemblance to Chopin, who cried into the face of death as it came down upon him, '*Merde!*' There was also a temptation to admire this present generation for its disdain of death....

But here a man would be wrong. What appears here to be courage in the face of death is merely mass-man apathy. What appears to be stoicism is merely the expression of the condition of mass-man: neither good nor bad, but basically and with a certain satisfaction at being so, nothing. I really do not know how to characterise the spiritual condition of my dreary contemporaries better than that.

Today, rumours are circulating of an uprising which has flared in Vienna. I do not believe that there is any real basis to it. Most likely, the story derives from the gossip and trotting about of a few market women, and that's about all. Mass-man moves, robotlike, from digestion to sleeping with his peroxide-blonde females, and produces children to keep the termite heap in continued operation. He repeats word for word the incantations of the Great Manitou, denounces or is denounced, dies or is made to die, and so goes on vegetating. And there is not even a blush when he is confronted by the legacy of his fathers, by the monuments of a noble past, by the crowning achievements of his own culture

But even this, the overrunning of the world with Neanderthals, is not what is unbearable. What is unbearable is that this horde of Neanderthals demands of the few full human beings who are left that they also shall kindly turn into cavemen; and then threatens them with physical extinction if they refuse.

We read in Heraclitus:

They no longer know that the many are always the evil and the few, the good. The Ephesians go so far as to force all the aged to hang themselves and leave the city to the youth. They have hunted Hermodor, who was the foremost among them, from the city with the cry, 'no one shall be called most virtuous amongst us – let him be so elsewhere and amongst others.'

December 1938

I rack my brains trying to discover the meaning of this persecution of the Jews which Goebbels has instigated.[33] At a time when this regime still urgently needs peace, surely this must call forth the deadly enmity of the whole world and make war inevitable. I cannot find the motivation, not even when I try to imagine myself a Nazi, and follow what I would imagine would be his train of thought.

I know that dictators must stage a new fireworks show every five months in order to hold the allegiance of the canaille.... This is what drove Napoleon III from Sevastopol to the Chinese Expedition, to Magenta, Solferino, Mexico, and finally, Sedan.

All this is incontrovertible, and might well explain the events of 9 November, if it were not for the fact that Hitler is also thereby bringing war down on himself – a war which he must certainly avoid if he is not to dig his own grave.

I discussed this with L., hard-working official at the Foreign Ministry, who simply laughed at me and my complicated analyses. His explanation of everything was Hitler's sudden fits of rage; now playing Artaxerxes, Hitler at once begins to roar when he does not immediately get his way, throws himself to the floor, and bites the carpet.

This is the reason, then, if L. is right, for all this misery and this immeasurable shame. But I wish to cite two cases, which took place before my eyes, so to speak. The first concerns a niece of Sonnenthal, the actor, who was driven from one refuge to the next, until finally, deathly tired, and beyond wanting to live any more, she simply walked up into the mountains on one of the first freezing nights of this autumn. After days of searching, we finally found her: she was dead.

The second story is even more shattering. I will not name its unfortunate subject for reasons that are highly personal. It was told me by the widow of our immortal Leo von Zumbusch:

Aged Fräulein X lived in great seclusion in her two-room apartment on Munich's Maximilianstrasse. A well-known actor who had managed to win great popularity with the Nazis decided that he wanted these two rooms. He found it unheard of for an old Jewish woman to be inhabiting them and denounced the old lady to get the apartment. This is tantamount to deportation to a concentration camp and slow death by starvation in these glorious times. Old Fräulein X knew this very well, and felt herself to be too old and too weak for this bitter path. She turned with an urgent plea for a quick-acting poison to the mother of one of her pupils.

The friend was a woman of character and determination. First, she offered every conceivable aid and protection to the old, weary lady. When this did not work, she had the courage to go to a Munich pharmacologist, a colleague of her husband's, to ask for the poison....

This gentleman, who to make matters worse was himself a follower of Hitler, was furious at the very idea, and at first refused. Then, however, as the utter hopelessness of the case was driven home to him, he overcame his sense of outrage sufficiently to slip a mixture of curarine and potassium cyanide into her hand. The lady returned to Fräulein X, really already a dying woman, with the poison.

And now it turned out that with her tearful thanks for the poison, Fräulein X had still one more request: would the friend sing Brahms' *Ernste Gesänge* before they parted? The friend, who is a singer, complied. She left, and today at lunch we got word that old Fräulein X had been found dead in her apartment. The man who had denounced her, the actor P., had grown impatient and was at her door at the time.

These were things I witnessed, so to speak. I give the names of the denouncers in neither case. In the Sonnenthal case, the individual is a 79-year-old one-time dancer, a Hitlerite now living in Vienna ... an old slattern who soon, on her deathbed, will see before her the Seat of Judgement....

And the other one?

I have now lived more than fifty years, have been forced to descend into certain dark places, and I have emerged with one piece of wisdom: no harm that I have ever done has not caused me pain later on, if it took decades. One way or another, sooner or later, often when it is almost forgotten, I wonder: is there now and then in the cocktails which Herr P. enjoys in his apartment acquired in this way the taste of a mixture of curarine and potassium cyanide ... and through the march music resounding out of his radio, does he not perhaps, at times, hear something like the *Ernste Gesänge*?

April 1939

With the passing of this endless winter, which really seemed to have adapted itself to what is generally meant by 'Nordic', I went again to Berlin. There was a great deal of bustle in connection with Hitler's birthday, and the approach of this national holiday was indicated by the fact that the hotels were flooded with the various storm, overstorm, tornado, and hurricane troopers which Germany has at its disposal. Their hideous boots were visible in front of all the doors.

First, I met Hans Albers,[34] and had tea with him in his no doubt incredibly expensive apartment overlooking the Tiergarten. He has filled the apartment with questionable antiques which he unquestionably thinks are genuine.

But he is a good fellow, if petrified with fear at the thought of getting old. Albers qualifies as one of the major celebrities of this part of the world, and in private is a simple and charming Hamburg type, but he has the same trouble as Kaiser Wilhelm II. The Kaiser was also easy and pleasant in tête-à-tête, but when he had to appear in public, he was unbearable. With me, however, Albers even exhibited a certain sentimentality, and he had tears in his eyes when he told me about his mother's attempt on her deathbed to sing the famous *Schleswig-Holstein, Sea Surrounded* of her native Holstein.

Berlin smells of war, and strikes me as looking the way a parvenu never should: shabby, wan, ridiculous. The menus offer little, the wine is even more questionable than usual, the linen is of doubtful cleanliness. The coffee is miserable, there is no petrol for

the taxis, and since repairmen have been drafted for work on forti-
fications, the hotels are in a sorry state. All kinds of things are now
visible under the plushy, stuccoed, bronzed junk which formerly
concealed the down-at-the-heels artifice which is Prussia's natural
style.

One evening, led on by a whispering, winking promoter, I
landed in an old Westside nightclub located in a basement.
Through Herr Göring, it stayed open until morning at which time,
in the best tradition of old Berlin, the waiters sat slumped and
exhausted at empty tables. During my visit, the place was filled to
capacity with young men of the rural nobility, all of them in SS
uniforms. They were evidently in Berlin to attend the approaching
Emperor's Birthday. The club was filled with the odour of their
bad cigarettes and their noisy manner, which was even worse.

They were having a fine time dropping pieces of ice from the
champagne coolers down the décolletages of their ladies and
retrieving the pieces of ice from the horrible depths amidst general
jubilation. They derided a doddering old man with a long white
beard who had wandered into this den for some unfathomable
reason, and generally communicated with each other in loud
voices that must certainly have been understandable on Mars, their
speech the pimps' jargon of the First World War and the Free
Corps period – the jargon which is what the language has become
during the last twenty years.

From my table, I examined their faces. They were the bearers of
old, blood-spattered names, they were the sons of beer-happy
fathers who were once, to the astonishment of their contemporaries, embassy councillors and attachés, bestowing upon the
world the Teutonic belly and dash of soccer stars – looking ludi-
crous and almost touching in their stern inflexibility and rigid
helplessness.

To observe these men meant looking at the unbridgeable abyss
that separates all of us from the life of yesterday. True, the beer-
bellies and the bags under the eyes are gone, the faces are lean and

narrow now. At first sight they look like a group of dragon-killers or like archangels who have left their wings in the cloakroom.... Until a second, harder look ... until the sound of this whorehouse jargon and the coarseness of their expressions bring quite a different analogy to mind.

The first thing is the frightening emptiness of their faces. Then one observes, in the eyes, a kind of flicker from time to time, a sudden lighting up. This has nothing to do with youth. It is the typical look of this generation, the immediate reflection of a basic and completely hysterical savagery.

I knew the old Kaiser's army. After a year or two of World War, it was gone. And I know that the Belgian atrocities charged against that army were based either on a tragic misunderstanding or on the propaganda needs of the adversary. Had that old army been ordered to carry out just one of the acts of conscious cruelty charged against it, the shooting down of a defenceless enemy, it would have mutinied! But woe to Europe if ever this hysteria that confronts us now gets free rein. These young men would turn the paintings of Leonardo into an ash heap if their Führer stamped them degenerate. They would not hesitate to send cathedrals tumbling into the air, using the hellish arts of I.G. Farben, if this were part of a given situation. Oh, they will perpetrate still worse things, and worst, most dreadful of all, they will be totally incapable of even *sensing* the deep degradation of their existence.

The next day in front of the Reich Chancellery, packed into the mob, deafened by the crash of drums, cymbals, and tubas of the marching troops, I witnessed the festivities. I heard the clamour, saw the enraptured faces of the women, saw, also, the object of this rapture.

There he stood, the most glorious of all, in his usual pose with hands clasped over his belly, looking, with his silver-decorated uniform and cap drawn far down over his forehead, like a tram conductor. I examined his face through my binoculars. The whole of it waggled with unhealthy cushions of fat; it all hung, it was all slack and without structure – slaggy, gelatinous, sick. There was no light in it, none of the shimmer and shining of a man sent by God. Instead, the face bore the stigma of sexual inadequacy, of the rancour of a half-man who had turned his fury at his impotence into brutalising others.

And through it all this bovine and finally moronic roar of '*Heil*!' ... hysterical females, adolescents in a trance, an entire people in the spiritual state of howling dervishes.

I went back to the hotel with Clemens von Franckenstein, whom I met accidentally today. We talked about my observations yesterday, and he reminded me that the German peerage register is full of listings of families like the von Arnims, Riedesels, von Kattes, von Kleists, and Bülows, with members holding positions such as 'Group Leader' and similar offices under this criminal.... These honours are accepted without a thought of the disgrace they thereby bring to the famed old names they bear, and to their forefathers. And I reflected again on this thick-witted mob and its bovine roar; on this failure of a Moloch to whom this crowd was roaring homage; and on the ocean of disgrace into which we have all sunk.

No, the much-maligned generation of the Wilhelms never quite reached this point of adoration of a Chosen One. In this case, it is really true that yesterday's sins were not as bad as today's. No, these are filth! These ceremonials are not anything to be seen and grasped. Satan has loosened his bonds, a herd of demons is upon us....

This people is insane. It will pay dearly for its insanity. The air of this summer is full of foreboding, and fire and iron must heal what no physician can any longer cure.

On the train back to Munich, D.[35] told me about the time in the First World War when he was Hitler's company commander. He described Hitler as a man constantly in a kind of daze. As company runner, he regularly and bravely marched 'into the jaws of death', but once out of danger he was generally considered the company fool by his comrades.

There is also an odd rumour, never quite dispelled, about the Iron Cross he wears.[36] I merely report it, since I lack the facts to verify it. An officer familiar with the procedure under which decorations were awarded at the time brought to my attention recently the fact that an award of the Iron Cross, First Class, was automatically accompanied by promotion to non-commissioned officer. This being so, the officer had come to the conclusion that this particular decoration was 'self-awarded'.

I do not like the ugly custom which has sprung up these past few years of nasty, uncritical backbiting. I will not do the same, and so I merely record what I have heard, without taking a position on the matter. The man has certainly *lied*, and not only in politics. He has lied regularly and often to enhance his own personal reputation. For example: on 9 November 1923, that legendary day, after Hitler had managed to get away from the Feldherrnhalle intact,[37] he concocted a fantastic story about a crying child he had tried to rescue from the whizzing bullets. No eyewitness saw the child. Undoubtedly, the purpose of the story was to cover his ignominious flight with a sentimental tear-jerker.

D. told me something else which characterises the man. Prior to the famous Assumption of Power, Hitler always addressed his former company commander with the formal 'you', and as 'Captain, sir', and D., whenever they met, used the familiar 'you' to his one-time runner....

Thus the usages of the First World War, which held until 1932. Now D. was a Munich attorney, and the other was the all-powerful man in the silver-threaded tram conductor's cap.... Now, this was the Moloch of the Germans, master over life and death – this former inhabitant of a Barerstrasse[38] furnished room, who had the boundless temerity recently to offer one of his gangland decorations (refused, with thanks) to the sovereign of a foreign state.[39]

But this is how it is with the dear Prussians, and even with this poor imitation Prussian: try as they may, they cannot hide their basic recruit mentality; not even when a caprice of fate wafts them into the places of power. Even as D. goes on talking, a troop of youngsters comes marching out into the muggy spring day in the street below. They are not carrying comfortable rucksacks, but duffelbags, on their backs. The bags carry less and pull bestially, but they have the advantage of being reminiscent of the barracks and parade ground. This is how they are. Well-packed and ready for use at any time in each blanket roll is their master sergeant's dream of how to order life, with which they have ruined Germany and which they now propose to present to the world. Very soon now, Germany will be faced with the ultimate question: whether to free itself from Prussian hegemony, or cease to exist. There is no third way.

The occasion of the Emperor's Birthday celebration in Berlin was also used to raise Herr Bruno Brehm[40] to the eminence of poet laureate: Herr Brehm, who first introduced himself to me as a monarchist of purest black-and-gold hue, and who two years later wrote that low book about the Kaiser during the war.... Herr Bruno Brehm who as late as 1930 was seeking favours in the antechambers of the literary Jews of Vienna; who dedicated his books 'in faithful recollection' to their equally Jewish wives; and who now, a few years later, writes one inflammatory anti-Semitic article after the other.

Oh, I am sure that he has some atrophied archduke safely tucked away somewhere ready for use as his political alibi the moment the wind changes. In any case, I know he will be more agile about changing course than Benno von Mechow, who became a Catholic in 1933, when it seemed as if the Catholics were going to win. This did not happen, however, and so he veered around to the Nazis. Unfortunately, this did not produce as powerful an effect on the Hitlerites as he might have wished.

But isn't this the way they all are? Are they not typified by the World War cadet who was never promoted, emerged from the war to write one powerful book based on powerful and unique experience, and then, faced with the fact that he lacked all ability to tell a story, was unable to complete a second book founded on fantasy and imagination? So they have served up the same old brew a third, a fourth, a fifth time, in book after book, merely by the addition of hot water, and without the brew getting any stronger, obviously. For years now they have done nothing but rewrite the same book under the guise of filling in the gaps in previous versions by their immense writer's craft.

Eternal cadets, old enough now to command a division; imitators of Hamsun, and of Adalbert Stifter; specialists in blood and soil, earth-smell and pipe-stink; pre-Raphaelite youths with Tyrtaeus eyes; archangels and dragon-killers of intact virginity and negative Wassermanns.

Not a whole-bodied man in the lot. Not one who has not had his 'little misdeed' as old Fontane called it in his Stine stories. Not one whom a man might call 'friend'.

I have said it before: for us who have remained, hardest of all to bear is our ever increasing loneliness. One after another, our comrades are disappearing, opponents as well as those who thought as we did.

Today, when I got off the train, I learned that Max Mohr is dead.

Emigrated in 1934, died while working as a doctor in Shanghai – a year ago; and I learn of his death only now. Officer of selfless bravery in World War I, skier and mountain-climber, farmer and physician.

Friend of David Herbert Lawrence. Author of the unforgettable *Improvisations in June* which told of the revolt by the romantics. Author, also, of two novels even more powerful, if that is possible, than that. No one so unsure and retiring on a pavement. No one so stoutly a man on a mountain top, and in the snow.

Lawrence and Mohr: were they not two soldiers in the newly formed troop of those who had seen through the stock-market world and were roused into action by their disgust? Were they not both of this little band as yet without a flag, as yet everywhere scattered – but which will never, so long as the sun continues to shine on this earth, so lose hold as to despair and sell itself?

From *Friendship of Ladiz*:

This was at a time when men did not yet have navels. There was such a time, of course, when there was no such thing. Navels were invented by the Prussians.... Probably out of their innate sense of order, so that a man would have a portable commemorative medal of the day of his birth!

No one ever so irresistibly ridiculed his own country, and no one so enfolded it in a tempestuous love. No one ever so charmingly administered a kick to the seat of the pants of everything and everybody we both hate: the Kurfürstendamm and I.G. Farben; the industrial knighthood of the Ruhr, the lads in knickerbockers of the Silberspiegel Club (the Silberspiegel was known as a homosexual club); and the old bridge-playing and philanthropic whores of the Berlin faubourgs.

Oh, Bavaria, my Bavaria, most beautiful of lands now in the great pause between the fourth and fifth acts of the drama of the distant Gods: the village street stands empty, it is the time of milking, to the south rises a fata morgana in chalk, *Karwendel*. Still farther, a black-clad procession moves through the fields: an old farmer being carried from his house, finished with living. A long and deep completion it has been, and without hurry. Now they carry him from the house of his birth and his completion, the neighbours carry him across to the little church with the onion-towers. And still farther away are other neighbours, now bringing in the hay. Heavy stallions pull the green-painted wagons, the last Bavarian stallions before the advent of the tractors, the steel dragons.

The light of the setting sun lies across these images – what is the secret, painful fear for your home that emerges here? The light of the setting sun lay across your youth as across mine when you gave me *Friendship of Ladiz* that ominous July of 1931.

Emigrated to Shanghai two years later, struck down by a heart attack far from his Karwendel birthplace; cremated abroad, his ashes strewn to the winds from the afterdeck of a ship in the North Sea, near home, off Helgoland....

Cut from a different pattern than these businessman-novelists, with their unflinching war stories and their marvellous cadets whose unruly lives end in 'the luck of a quick death, which all of us want, finally'.

Now you, also. A light goes out, and then another. Finally, the theatre is dark, and the stage, where all was light and animation only a short time before, is empty. Every now and then, an icy wind sweeps out of the dark rooms behind, into the stage.

Courage is required to go on living now. Courage, and a daily summoning-up of all one's will. For years now, to go on living has been to go on hating. Courage is needed, and belief in that idea struggling so hard to become reality.

August 1939

I have been at Jannings', on the Wolfgangsee. His impressive estate now lies deep under a shadow – its owner's fears about a war. He is preoccupied with fear about what will happen to his art collection and his stocks and bonds, and about next year's supply of coal for the central heating of his house, and about whether there will be a sufficient variety of sausage for his dinner the coming year. As a performer, he is neither more nor less than a character actor of the first magnitude; as a man, he is a fat bourgeois whose fears about the coming world storm centre about whether his siesta with fishing pole and cigar on the shores of the lake will be seriously disturbed.

Jannings told me all kinds of things about the famous Berlin scandal involving Goebbels, who was supposed to have been found in tête-à-tête with the wife of the actor, Fröhlich, and soundly beaten by the latter. The truth is somewhat different – unfortunately. Since Jannings says he was an actual eyewitness, I will vouch for the truth of his version.

It seems that Herr Fröhlich left a party in Jannings' company, and went to get his car to drive home. Fröhlich found his wife in the car, together with the Herr Minister ... in, let us say, tête-à-tête. He did not challenge Herr Goebbels, but later slapped his wife several times and thanked his valet for helping him expose his adulterous wife.

This is the true story. The man could not find the courage, quite, for any public action. But the popular version insists on a more gratifying ending to the story, and holds fast to its vision of the beaten Cabinet Minister. Suddenly, a song entitled 'I Want To Be Happy' ('*Ich möchte einmal fröhlich sein*') has become immensely popular.

I have been spending the last few days of August on the Chiemsee with Herr von K., who was a cabinet member years ago, and who as a young man knew Bismarck. We talked about his experiences during the war, and about the first days of the war twenty-five years ago on the East Prussian border. Then, just before the declaration of war and on nights of a full moon, the patrols would trot back and forth at the edges of the fields, one man behind the other, carefully avoiding the heavy stalks of grain. Even after the war had begun, it was hard to get the peasant recruits to overcome their feelings and ride into the wheat fields ready for harvest....

Images from a world so near in time, yet already become like a legend from the past: A Prussian dragoon plunges his lance into the body of a Russian during the first cavalry battle, knocking him from his horse. He cannot pull the lance out of the body. Suddenly, looking down at the Russian, he begins to cry bitterly. The Russian strokes his hand, telling him not to take it to heart, for *Christ's sake*.

Another image: A little Jewish boy, condemned to death under martial law for aiding the enemy, is being led to execution and does not understand. He is handed an order on which the verdict is written, glances at it uncomprehendingly and asks: 'Please ... for what is the little paper?'

Another: A little old Russian peasant who was wearing the uniform of the Russian Army when captured told us that he and his comrades were quite ready to shoot when the range was a thousand metres or more ('You can't hit a thing.'). And even when the range had narrowed to five hundred metres, they fired ('At least, you can't see whether you've hit or not.'). But when the Germans had got to within one hundred metres, all the Russians threw away their guns, and under no circumstances used them – 'Because who, sir, would take on himself to sin at such close range!'

Then we talked about Bismarck, while Herr Hitler's heavily loaded military convoys rolled eastward on the Salzburg highway below. As a young man in the foreign service, K. was to give a lecture before the Chancellor. On Bismarck's desk was a plate containing a chunk of sausage, and from time to time, as the young men delivered their little speeches, the old glutton would cut himself a slice as thick as a thumb, cover it with a piece of butter again as thick, and bite into it, without troubling about bread....

There is no doubt in my mind that the physical durability of a chief of state has a profound effect on the policies it follows. The rise and fall of Napoleon's empire is an example. And I would like to know what catastrophe would ensue if the Chief Eunuch now deciding the fate of Germany were ever to sit down to just one of these Bismarckian snacks.

I would be a spiritual cripple if I attempted to deny Bismarck's real stature and emotional depth. But we are now reaping the harvest of the industrially overdeveloped Greater Prussia whose seeds he sowed. I am more than ever convinced that his work contains the fatal flaw of a great man's tragic misjudgement, and that it is this we have to thank for this government of industry-minded dolts, and for the fact that we are being overrun by the masses, who reproduce like rabbits, have no work to keep them occupied, and are therefore made all the more greedy for power.

We are on the threshold of a second world war, in which again all of geography will be against the Germans, and which will derive from the Bismarckian state. And I am quite sure that such a war, declared by the eternal Prussian as it will be, is lost before the first shot is fired. We will not be able to talk about better days until we have before us the outlines of the coming catastrophe. This perspective we will have only when we are sitting atop the relatively small pile of rubble which will result from the relatively short war to come – a war which is inevitable, and which will break out *soon*.

Already there is a touch of autumn about this crystal-clear day, the last day of peace. With the measured precision of stars, a span of oxen pulls the plough uphill and downhill over a field unchangeable, looking exactly as they did when they lowed over the cradle of Christ. The clean and entirely innocent landscape lies before me, open and peaceful, and solitary as the illustration in a book.

And yet havoc is in the air. People here sense it and are deeply troubled. The farmers, and more especially the Bavarian farmers, are the only people left in Germany who still keep contact with their own inner being and basic sense of reality, despite the universal hysteria and the series of successful political robberies. The only enthusiasts in the village are the Hitler Youth rowdies who were trained in Radau and have an idea that the war is going to be like the Austrian and Czech *promenades militaires*.

The next morning, as I was on my way home, the blacksmith came out to tell me the news: the pygmies to whom Germany's fate is now linked have taken the leap, and at this very moment that power-drunk schizophrenic's voice is crackling out of every loudspeaker.

I pressed the man's hand. For what will soon be seven years, he has suffered and hated as I have. I have no doubt that immeasurable suffering is coming, and that it could not be avoided. But I also have no doubt about the thing that has sustained me for six years, and maintained me in the darkest hours of my life ... the certainty that today the great monster signed his own death warrant.

I have hated you in every hour that has gone by, I hate you so that I would happily give my life for your death, and happily go to my own doom if only I could witness yours, take you with me into the depths. When I let this hate free, I am almost overcome by it, but I cannot change this and do not really know how it could be otherwise. Let no one deprecate this, nor fool himself about the power of such hatred. Hate drives to reality. Hate is the father of action. The way out of our defiled and desecrated house is through the command to hate Satan. Only so will we earn the right to search in the darkness for the way of love.

20 September 1939

So the Nazis (I do not want to speak of the *Germans* in this connection) ... the Nazis are conquering, and what else is one to expect? A hopelessly rainy summer has been followed by a clear, sunny autumn, full of the smoky perfumes of that season, with the ground solid and hard-packed and as though made to order for those tanks to roll over and flatten to earth whatever stands in their way ... the Polish Cavalry, the whole Polish Army ... and if Poland is ours today, tomorrow it must be the whole world.

Yes, the Nazis are conquering and perhaps internally even more than on the battlefield. The editors exult in bloodthirsty fashion on the newsprint into which our forests are to be converted. They have invented a brand-new language to match the great times in which we live, and now proclaim the Realisation of 1899, and the Commitment of the Woman at War, and the Reinforcement by the German Woman, and talk about that ancient piece of German ground, Posen. And when they are reminded that Posen was Polish territory as far back as the time of Frederick the Great, and that even earlier soldiers from Danzig fought on the Polish side in the First Battle of Tannenberg, they turn nasty and threaten to tell the Gestapo....

The Nazis are, indeed, conquering, and their 'war commentators' bring new glory to the German language, as they 'shower the enemy with sparks enough to make him burn for peace' and 'give him something to chew on that lays him flat on the ground'. And when they are told that their German is the German of the latrine wall and the pimp, they turn very nasty indeed, and roar that they are soldiers, and that this happens to be how soldiers talk, and if you don't believe it, you can find out in a concentration camp.

Oh, yes, the Nazis do nothing but conquer, they conquer just as uninterruptedly as Wilhelm's armies did in 1914, and the beer-hall regulars again have the entire world annexed. And in the local café, recently, the old one-time Medical Corps general employed the current jargon in lumping Poles and Englishmen together as 'pigs' – despite the fact that the old man never in his life saw an example of the latter in his 'natural habitat', so to speak.

When I rose and objected to such entirely uncalled-for language, he looked at me with the eyes of a wounded stag, felt that the world had collapsed at his feet, and mumbled something about how he had always thought I was a *patriotic* man.

22 September 1939

Dear Reck,

I am writing from home, back from the Polish War and before I leave for the Western Front of this Second World War. I am now a captain in the Air Force, and am just back from the Battle of Poland and eleven flying missions – some of them rather unusual missions like dive-bombing columns of troops and troop trains. Once, out of sheer love of the craft, I wangled an invitation as a 'guest' on a bombing run over Warsaw – one of many such, of course, but this was a vertical dive from 16,000 feet down to 2,200. And I came out of it untouched, even if there are a few scratches on the crate. And now for England. But more of that later.

You heard right: I'm not lying, we are about to dare the impossible. We are the children of the gods, and they are most merciful. But we have our own way of tempting fate: we put our hands around its throat and say, 'Bless me, or I won't let go!'

Dear Reck, I have not written to you for many years now. But we have time enough and to spare, we humans, we do not need to hurry. I have wanted to come clear about my preference for East Prussia and whether it was somehow too hasty. Now, I have flown over it all, from its northern extremity completely across the whole of it, to attack the enemy, and each time with a bomb-load of 1,600 kilos. And each time I have come back a couple of hours later from the Polish wastes safe and sound to the glory of Masuria. Sometimes, there were dead on board, planes were missing, or a crate was so shot up it could only be landed in a heap of twisted metal. Because, when you have caught a Polish infantry transport battalion on the southern edge of a swamp, and left it a quarter-hour later a burial ground, you do not ask yourself what price you paid, and you feel that your own death would be incommensurate. I do not know, Reck, how well you know the Polacks, or how enduring you consider that the Order we have created here will be. But this much I do know: this Order will remain, *even if Europe, and England too, has to be turned into ruins and ashes.*

I was a member of the Hitler Youth, I was granted a post of some authority despite the fact that I was not a war veteran, and I am, naturally, a bone-deep believer in National Socialism. Yes, Reck, I know about the terrible mistakes that were made. There are places where the dry rot reaches right down into the ground. But I know also that these mistakes are not fatal – rather, that fate accompanies the spirit, precisely in the sense expressed by my great friend, Reck-Malleczewen, and that I can confidently believe in the spirit of my Third Reich. We two, you and I, move in directions that are completely opposed, of course. Austria, the Sudetenland, Bohemia, Memel were Christmas presents for me. Then, in midsummer, and even now, in the middle of the war, the mere thought that Vienna is no longer apart from the German Reich gives me a feeling of physical well-being. And the war against Poland was my war, long awaited, long desired, and fought with passion. I was glad to take part in it. Eleven times I took leave of this East Prussian glory and flew over fields dotted with ten thousand girls waving good-bye; and eleven times I came back, deeply happy, larger than life. Now the war must be carried against England, so that East Prussia can be released from its isolation and its cage of boundary lines, once and for all. A difficult task. I believe that England is either an article of faith, or a superstition. It may prove to be a tough piece of leather to work. But to win in 1918 at incredible cost, and then in 1933, or certainly by 1935, to allow one's adversary to become powerful once again – surely, this is political dilettantism of the most ridiculous kind! And then, only then, war with Germany? No, Reck, that is simply nonsense, gross stupidity, parliamentary umbrella politics which lets every favourable chance go by, and then challenges the adversary when you feel personally insulted.

I haven't the slightest idea what is going to happen from now on. Mind at rest, I merely sit in my bombing-crate and shoot down anybody who gets in the way. But I am beginning to get the idea that the issue that has to be fought out here is simply the total existence of either England or Germany. Reck, I don't care how many warnings there are about 'darkening skies' and England. We are not unaccustomed to fighting in the dark. Remember that we have gained priceless experience in Poland on how to deal with peoples and nations which insist on being our enemies. The Poles certainly fought with remarkable courage. Still, we quite pitilessly shot them to pieces. I believe that we did not even hate the Poles – certainly we don't now, completely demoralised mass of primitives that they are today. Still, when there is a question of German farmers being shot in the back, we are going to deal with the matter in a completely new spirit of Germanic coldness, no matter if we have to put any number of Polish intellectuals against the wall. And what is certain here is that the most important of these are already gone, and that in case of emergency there are always more German farmhands available than there are Polish intellectuals. I don't know if methods like these are adaptable for England. But what I *am* certain about is that we are slowly coming around to acting in the spirit of: 'If you will not be my brother, your head will be dropped off your shoulders.' I have solemnly concluded that I will strike down any member of any nation who infringes on our newly created New Order in the East, or in any way tries to do damage to National Socialism. And I will do this with a pitilessness that should provide food for thought. I am not inclined to wish an attack of softheartedness on Germany, until this battle ends in either death or life as a people. Certainly the English, in their arrogant declaration of a war of hunger on women and children, have shown what they think of compassion and humanity.

Does this horrify you, Reck? But I have never forced either the Czechs or the Poles to be our implacable enemies, and now that England has chosen this moment to declare war on us, I am merely being logical when I reject shuddering and hand-wringing as a means of waging war. This new World War undoubtedly goes sharply against the grain of many people, but I have no doubt that there are several tens of thousands of my type who will *force* the rest to perform the way they should.

I expect that we will carry on the war against England with the same icy-cold mathematical reasoning ... quite differently from the hazy, hit-or-miss quality of Wilhelm's war. It is wonderful that despite the exhaustion following the First World War, this nation can now be brought by its leadership into a new and considerably more grim war situation. By comparison, I believe the English people have been more or less enervated by too much city living, that they are hardly capable of heroism, and that, with the exception of the old aristocracy, their culture is worthless. The German, of course, is hardly different, and little remains of the old aristocracy, but he has, instead, a new dream. Anyway, it will be a proper carnage, and if I next find myself turned into a rocket falling from the heavens, I will still, at the last moment, acknowledge this much: we have had our share of the fun.

So. I have spoken. All the best.

Your X.X.

A letter written by a thug, an escaped convict? No, that letter was written by a young man with lively blue eyes and the irresistible laugh of a boy, a good fellow who in civilian life was entirely harmless ... a young man of good Rhineland middle-class stock, of a certain tradition, of certain pretensions to culture. But this is the result of all these painless victories and this 'National-Socialist

piety'. The 'crate' may be a little 'scratched', but a man never hesi-
tates about flying right past God's nose, announcing: 'I will not let
go; bless me. If you don't, we will come with an entirely new,
German coldness, and put a number of angels against the wall.'

This is the meaning of these victories. This is the tone, this is the
pimps' jargon which now croaks out of every loudspeaker and
flows from the pens of the newspaper thugs-in-uniform. And do
not dare to contradict, or it's the Gestapo for you. And children
denounce their parents, and brothers, if there's a little something
in it for them, deliver up their sisters, and all in all, what is right is
what is useful for Germany....

And the effect to be achieved by this total war is the total
flooding of the earth with this new generation of Germans, and if
not enough new Germans are produced ... why, there is even
provision for this eventuality in the efficiency of the German
order.

A young couple in Munich recently discovered that a defect of
vision, with recurrent blindness, seemed to be hereditary in the
man's family. The young man had himself sterilised forthwith. But,
since as good Germans, they were obligated to have children, the
husband unflinchingly sent his wife to the Fount of Youth.[41] The
Fount is an SS organisation, with offices in the remains of the syna-
gogue on Lenbachplatz.

Available at the offices of the Fount is an album of the photos of
guaranteed-pedigree, Nordic blonde SS men. The client chooses
one of these according to taste, and then indicates her choice of
stud to the Fount official. Soon thereafter the client finds herself
pregnant, and in due course the mother of a little Germanic Pan,
named Heinz-Dieter or Eike. And this little fellow will grow up to
strike down, with a completely new and unusual German coldness,
everything which dares to infringe on the New German Order or
National Socialism.

All this is taken care of by the Fount of Youth, 13 Lenbachplatz,
Munich. Telephone number so-and-so. German blood will out,

even out of a brothel!

This is what we have come to, then, and this is the life of a people winning one victory after another.

Frankly, I do not believe there is an ideology behind all this. I believe neither in Founts of Youth nor little Germanic Pans; neither in dragon-killer eyes, nor in cherubic cheeks; neither in the retouched blonde braids of BDM girls demonstratively bouncing off their shoulders ('Look! See how healthfully country-style we are!'), nor in the drums of the Hitler Youth. I believe neither in the New German Order, nor in this whole Wotan and Germanic gods business – in the midst of a people which is sixty per cent part-Slavic.... And the Wotan they are talking about probably came into the world in a Leipzig suburb as the son of a Teutonic-minded fencing instructor, while his Edda will turn out to be a high-school teacher from Schkeuditz, Saxony.

No, based on a perspective gained by many years of watching them, I say that all this comes down to colossal self-deception, behind which lurk all the inclinations of fettered masses: greed and resentment, looseness, and rut, and sexual libertinism, and a complete closing-off of the individual, not just from God but from the *gods*. The mobs in the cities during the decline of the Roman Empire showed the same drive to be considered a 'young people', the same belligerent uproar, the same challenging of other nations; then too, whatever demands were made, the rest of the world must accede, because this is how it is with a young nation!

In actual fact, what we have here are irremediably sick and futureless mass-men, whose ideal is amorphousness, whose ethos is formlessness, and who hate nothing so much as discipline, form, definition. It may very well be that responsibility for all of this is largely to be attributed to the businessmen and industrialists, great and small, of the turn of the century and postwar years, who gave impetus to the process by which this largely uprooted people huddled together to make a mass-man ant heap. It may have seemed to these leaders at that moment that the most satisfactory populace would be a mass of primitives. And the setting up of pseudo ideologies and symbolic pap – Wotan cults amidst the dynamos, kettledrums amidst the loudspeakers, Founts of Youth amidst VD clinics, and monkey-gland doctors – would be the most comfortable way of distracting attention from the real social and economic problems of the times.

In any case, Germany has been sinking deeper and deeper into unreality ever since.... It is now completely drugged on its own lies. The cure will be more awful than anything ever seen before in history.

One must hate Germany now, truly and bitterly, in order once again, if only for the sake of its glorious past, to be able later to enfold it in all of one's love – like a parent with his misguided and unfortunate child.

November 1939

I am writing this in Munich, which is still reeling from the attempted assassination[42] in the Bürgerbräukeller. The newspapers are weeping crocodile tears about the 'cowardly, murderous gangsters' who dared attack the 'greatest German of all time'. But there are, I think, probably no more than a thousand native Munichers who are not dejected because the attempt failed. The journalists joke cynically about their own articles. The official version has it that Otto Strasser placed the bomb for the British Intelligence Service. This has produced loud laughter. No one doubts that the whole display is a bit of pyrotechnics set off by the Nazis themselves. The fireworks cost nearly a dozen lives, but they serve to whip up hatred against the English and to provide Herr Hitler with the halo of a martyr.

I knew Otto Strasser only through his letters. Despite his Bavarian origins, he began calling himself a 'Prussian Jacobin' in the confusion of 1932, and pursued me throughout the entire summer of that year with indecent political proposals. His brother, Gregor, who was killed in the Röhm Putsch, was an honest chap, though he liked to hear himself talk. He came to see me several times in the late autumn of 1932, when it seemed that his star was rising, and I have him to thank for my knowledge of what happened behind the scenes as 1932 passed into 1933. I will never forget something he said that November, when the vote in the elections had gone against the Nazis, for the first time, after all their triumphs.

'He is talking about suicide to frighten his apostles,' Strasser said. 'He is such a hysteric that they need not take him seriously, and so he will not carry out his threat unfortunately. But it is all or nothing for him now. If I know him, he will make one desperate attempt to get into power. If this fails and he does not get his way, he is finished. He will burst into pieces like a frog.'

Gregor Strasser paid with his life, in the Röhm Putsch, for his opposition. I understand his severed and rotting corpse was found in a cornfield. It is typical of the spiritual state of the German people that when his children were told of the death of their father, the reaction of one was: 'He (Hitler) had father shot, but still, he is our Führer.' The wife of Strasser's friend Glaser[43] (Glaser was killed at the same time in his apartment on Munich's Amalienstrasse) had a very similar comment to make about the death of her husband.

I have spent a week at Hechendorf on the Pilsensee, visiting my friend Clemens von Franckenstein. Just two weeks before the war, Clé conducted a concert in London, and was the guest of Winston Churchill. Those were restoring days for me in the house of my old friend, with the lake melancholy in the late autumn. We talked about the letters, just published, which Stephan George wrote to Hugo von Hofmannsthal, and the incredible arrogance they revealed. I told Clé the details of an audience with George, when the writer, enthroned in an elevated armchair between two silver candlesticks, had asked me for my views on Aristotle: and how, two hours later, I saw King Stephan in Heidelberg, fat dripping from his mouth as he tore with truly Gargantuan zeal into his roast ribs of beef and sauerkraut in the second-class waiting room of the railroad station.

And we talked about the curious and almost unbelievable letter in which Herr Hans Pfitzner complained to German theatre directors – that he, the German master, was being neglected, while Verdi, that 'composer of brutal and blood-soaked works', was constantly being played....

An interesting comparison: Pfitzner, that ponderous, amateurish composer of amusing music, and Verdi ... that he dared to name himself in the same breath and on the same piece of paper with a musical giant whose music streamed forth as effortlessly as his breathing!

We talked for a long time about Pfitzner, about the rose-coloured paper flowers which he caused to rain onto the opera stage in his *Rose vom Liebesgarten*, and about the poison in the second act of his *Palestrina*. I sat in at one of the endless rehearsals for the latter at the Munich Hoftheater. Paul Gräner noticed Pfitzner slinking about the theatre, eyeing the seated spear-carriers, singers, and assorted supernumeraries, with his nasty school-teacher's look. 'He is writing down the name of everybody who laughs,' Gräner said.

Pfitzner also had a habit of changing instrumentalists' music. Once he found, above music written for the oboe, the word 'garbage'. He rushed to the director and demanded the immediate dismissal of the musician. It hardly helped when the oboist was punished with a fine of just five marks 'for the benefit of the pension fund'.

A violinist at the Berlin Opera told me that recently Pfitzner, having conducted a Verdi aria, at a concert, interrupted the spontaneous applause, saying, 'Do not laugh. It is only organ-grinder music.' It is entirely logical that Pfitzner, that painstakingly mediocre musical watchmaker, should hate the endlessly bountiful talent of a Verdi with the virulence of a dwarf.

I have known Clé for almost thirty years ... ever since those brilliant days when he was named director of the Royal Theatre, under the reign of the old Regent. The way the Nazis removed him from this office in 1934 is instructive. One day, Herr Christian Weber[44] arose in the Munich City Council and declared that the Munich Opera could no longer be considered a culturally significant institution, and that changes must be made. As evidence of the present spiritual state of the German people, I provide herewith a comparative summation of the critic and the object of his criticism....

Herr Clemens von Franckenstein

Career: Composer of operas in the repertoires of various opera houses and known as a conductor throughout the world. Dismissed from his post.

Address: A small and modestly furnished villa in the Westpol section of Munich.

Herr Christian Weber

Career: Prior to delivering his judgement on the state of the Munich Opera, bouncer at the Blue Boar tavern; convicted several times of assault. As a crony of Hitler, now, president of the Munich Racing Association, and owner of a flourishing whorehouse on Senefelderstrasse, Munich.

Address: The Munich Residenz, in palatial surroundings occupied by Pope Pius VI in 1782....

As a further note on the Third Reich, the following is now forbidden by the Führer's orders:[45]

1. Discussion of the private life, past or present, of high Nazi officials.

2. Any presentation of factual evidence before a court in a criminal case which might possibly cast an unfavourable light on one of these newly created demigods.

But in the *Public Defamer* this verse appears:

> The grain has gone to seed,
> Transformed are the nations,
> Our lives are a degradation
> While the bad boys laugh.
> What has happened before
> Has become true once more:
> The good have disappeared,
> The bad are everywhere.
> Once this misery is
> Broken as is ice,
> People will speak of it
> As of the Black Death.
> Then the boys on the moor
> Will make a figure of straw,
> Will turn pain to delight,
> And the old horror into light.

This poem, written by old Gottfried Keller in a moment of almost uncanny pre-vision of things to come, is the most popular of Keller's ballads in Germany today. Everyone knows it, everyone reads it aloud – as a matter of fact, I heard it at Steinicke's Tavern in Schwabing, read by old Steinicke himself to his astonished customers. The Gestapo is in a fury, but it cannot send a poem to a concentration camp, nor even stop its circulation. We have not yet come to where we can be forbidden to listen to a ballad by Keller.

January 1940

Unity Mitford, of whom I have spoken before, has committed suicide. She tried first to shoot herself in a Munich hotel. But she only managed to wound herself. Then, taken back to London, she was more successful with poison and died there. It was the most sensible thing the lady, who saw herself as the Queen of Germany alongside our Adonis, could have done. Seriously, and with all due respect for the dead, male hysterics do quite enough damage when they get into history. But females who manage to get up on the heights are even worse. And worst of all among them is the would-be saviour type. We have enough of this species, titled 'Nazi-esses' by the man in the street. England has another class of this genus, a type of female who clutches Herr Gandhi's white loincloth. The English should be thankful that there is one fewer, at least.

In the interim, we have a new scandal making the rounds in Munich. This one concerns Herr Fischer,[46] 'Managing Director' of Herr Hitler's very own Operettenhaus theatre on the Gärtnerplatz. Fischer is also a protégé of Gauleiter Wagner,[47] and as such is richly hated by Eberstein,[48] the Munich police chief, who is Wagner's deadly enemy.... Herr Fischer dined recently with an extremely young lady in the Regina Hotel, and slyly reserved a double room for the night. They went upstairs around midnight.... Shortly thereafter, a piercing cry for help rang out down the floor. Everyone rushed to the scene, and two young men from the adjoining rooms dashed inside. They found the young lady wearing pyjamas, in a state of considerable disarray, while Herr Fischer wore nothing but his ring. The maiden exclaimed tearfully that though she was 'not quite fifteen', Herr Fischer had tried to *rape* her, and she then proceeded to describe Herr Fischer to his face in terms used especially in the Giesing suburb of Munich.

The two men who had come to the rescue now revealed themselves to be members of the Gestapo, and Herr Fischer was arrested on the basis of the girl's cry and her 'tender age'. The rest I was told by the owner of the Regina: the girl and the Gestapo agents were all under orders from Eberstein, who hoped in this way to compromise and eliminate at least one of his enemy's followers; and this ass promptly sauntered into the neat little trap. He is now supposed to appear at the prosecuting attorney's office, and after that to be whisked off the scene, but I doubt that this will happen. Almost certainly, he will rise corklike to the surface of this rich brew of sewage and blood and tears again. Suddenly there he will be, rejuvenated and cleansed of sin. And the whole process will take as little time as it did to rehabilitate the head of the Nazis' motor transport corps, Oldenbourg,[49] who was supposed to go to jail for profiteering in cognac.

Herr Julius Streicher,[50] the Third Reich's great helden-tenor of anti-Semitism, was convicted by a jury of his Gauleiter peers for having taken bribes from rich Nuremberg Jews. Rumour was that he had been shot, but I was convinced from the start that not a hair of his head would be touched. Just as I predicted, Streicher, who committed perjury a couple of years before the Assumption of Power, came through safe and sound. He now rules over the estate he acquired, God knows how, and he is supposed to stay there.

The latest is that the Great Man himself now has a mistress, named Eva Braun. Of course, we all know what the circumstances are, and the lady should really be described as a *maîtresse en titre*. She has been installed in one of the luxury villas erected on the Obersalzberg by her lover, close enough to be accessible at any time. There she plays at being First Lady of the Third Reich, if not Empress, dispenses chastisement and grace with fine impartiality, and is much sought after for her good offices by suppliants threatened by concentration camp. A prankish official who eavesdropped on a long-distance telephone conversation between the two of them has reported that Hitler figuratively cried on the blonde bosom of his girlfriend about the huge quantities of hormones and injections of vitamins being put into him. *Nota bene*: there is a complete harem of young girls on the Obersalzberg, who attend on Great Caesar exactly as their forerunners did on Bockelson. Like the young David who played on his lyre for Saul when that monarch was depressed, these girls dance for the King – who was formerly resident of a furnished room on Barerstrasse, in Munich – when he feels unhappy.

As with Bockelson, these young girls come almost entirely from families of Prussian nobility. They were procured and are presented in tasteful array before Divine and August Caesar by the procuress Frau von D., who was formerly secretary of the now renamed Herrenklub, in Berlin. Perhaps, when the inevitable cleansing of this Augean stable begins, we might start by rerouting everything belonging to this harem in the direction it should have taken: toward the South American bordellos.... And how would it be if at the same time the noble families who have allowed their names to be soiled by membership in the SS, the Gestapo, and the SA were removed forever from the Register of Nobility?

I am a conservative, but I declare that the coming revolution will give Germany its very last chance to put its house in order. If it lets this chance go by too, it will remain forever what it now is and what its bourgeois has been for a long time – a cesspool. And I include in this designation all of the Prussian nobility, with a few notable exceptions.

Our German Pericles has also been involved in another little matter, the suicide of his niece in 1930.[51] It has never been explained why the girl should have taken her own life in his quarters on Prinzregentenstrasse shortly before Christmas of that year. There are people who claim that the girl had been having an affair with a Jew, and shot herself out of guilt and fear.... But there are hints of other things. It appears that even at that time a great deal was covered up, that even under the Weimar Republic there were officials in the police department and the prosecuting attorney's office who were ready to help the 'coming man' with little services of this kind.

October 1940

Now, I am at Villach for the cure, and daily go to the springs at Lake Faaker, the Alps rising just beyond. The landscape here, with its Slavic *je ne sais quoi* and its autumnal melancholy, reminds me of a border region in Masuria: a southern, mountain-walled version of that other land's sad desolation: the chemical-bright hues of the girls' kerchiefs burning like eyes into the landscape; the filthy little restaurants where salads are made with machine oil because of the war; and the pathetic poverty and insufficiency of a border area covering everything and everybody like a film. This, despite the fact that prosperous East Tyrol is quite close by.

The hotel room where I sleep and have to stay in bad weather has the smell of the Balkans about it. A man in a well-cut suit is almost enough to stop the traffic.

The spa area is full of men taking the cure. Many of them have the lock of hair falling over the forehead that is characteristic of the Viennese house superintendent ... the same hair style affected by our Gypsy Baron. And their speech, as one hears it from the dressing-room adjoining, has the ring of the Balkans about it too: the price of pork, transactions in corn, women. Sometimes a joke about Hitler. But that is exceptional. People do not pay too much attention to him here, in this border region.

And now all the memories of this apocalyptic summer flood back. I recall now those days in early summer when bearded old grandfathers crowded about as the bulletins of victories were posted, their eyes glittering with greed and joy. It never entered their heads that a victory by Hitler would change unrecognisably their world of the moderate rental and payment-when-due morality. I see it all again, a whole people drunk on the success of a series of political robberies, thundering approval in the movies when the newsreels pictured burning men: a bloodthirsty mob roaring rapturously at the sight of human torches plummeting out of exploding tanks. There they all are before my eyes: beer-soaked old pinochle players dividing up continents over their steins: the post office clerks rolling their eyes at each other when the greeting is not 'Heil Hitler'; the stenographers promenading in silk stockings stolen in France by their boyfriends; the heroes on leave filling the air with stories about how they made their shaving cream from the froth of champagne....

The enthusiasm of 1914 was nothing compared to this – those pastors' wives distributing thin sandwiches on the steps of troop trains during the First World War were really giving expression to a most understandable fear. People saw disaster coming at them through every door and window. They tried to drown their fears in shouting exhilaration over rolling troop trains and the smooth perfection of the mobilisation machinery.

What is happening this time is something else. It is malevolent, crafty, bandit-like. Bourgeois Germany of 1914 had no idea of the game of roulette that was then beginning, in which the generals and industrial speculators would frivolously stake human lives. People then still had something of the old reliable uprightness of their middle-class past ... something of a soul. Today, that is buried beneath muck and sewage and blood, but I still believe in it, and pray daily to see it reappear.

What is happening here is something else, of which the grimmest manifestation is certainly the total absence of identification with the fighting. All people care about is the booty from these gigantic raids. In 1870, at least, legends arose about the cavalry battles around Metz. Sedan must have affected people as a powerful drama, despite the war-poster paintings of the time.

But no sparkling squadrons of cavalry gallop forth today. To a large extent, battles are now matters of movements back and forth of standardised machines. It may well be that this complete mechanisation of war has a great deal to do with the complete idiocy of those who look on at it. You turn the knob of your radio, and are served up gigantic wheelings of armies. You forget entirely about the daring and alertness required of the strategists, you hear only the boom from the loudspeakers. What you know about is, perhaps, the death of somebody on your side in a particular episode, and for the rest, about the silk stockings which Hiesl sent Theresa from Tourcoing, or about the cognac which some Army paymaster 'liberated' from France and which is now drunk in all the bars from coffee cups.

Wellington's words at Waterloo were part of Prussian legend for a hundred years thereafter, and of Sedan there remained the image of an unfortunate Emperor who tried unsuccessfully to find death on the battlefield, and then presented his dagger à *son chere cousin*. But this time – what really will remain in people's minds of the breakthrough at this latest Battle of Sedan, which ushered in the French tragedy? Or the taking of the Somme line?

Nothing ... I am certain that three weeks from now not one of the eight hundred people who were in that movie house with me will be able to associate the names of the places with the battles they saw. It is an old theory of mine that gasoline has done far more harm to mankind than alcohol, and I am sure that the masses in the United States or England react just as little to what happens to them as the Germans. But it is shattering when this Hottentot condition happens to one's own people. The average German now registers developments as he would the scores of the Sunday football games, shouts happily over the results and has forgotten all about them by next morning. He has got into the habit of victory, and takes each successive triumph more and more for granted, which is charmingly simple of him – except that he is becoming more and more brutalised, and the level of his greed is constantly going up. I can hear the rumbling of a terrible storm in the distance.

Truly, with the Germans it is as I have said: every nation normally puts its demons, its delusions, its impossible desires away into the cellars and vaults and underground prisons of its unconscious; the Germans have reversed the process, and have let them loose. The contents have escaped like the winds out of Pandora's box. A storm is raging across this long-suffering old earth. Germany, drunk with victory, is sick. The language one hears, the speech of the war commentators, the talk in the coffee-houses, together with the German of the military, has degenerated into a kind of street jargon that makes the blood run cold. The newspapers heap coals of fire on the banished Kaiser because he supposedly blocked a plan to have London erased from the map by a gigantic fleet of zeppelins in 1916. Little receptionists cry for blood, and old ladies who still have the aura of a better time now use slang to describe enemy statesmen that would make a Hamburg bartender stare.

And behind it all are the 'deals'. People sell stolen paintings and sculptures and wine cellars, which may or may not exist ... they 'deal' in securities, silk stockings, ownerless French factories – with stolen machines, with soup spoons, toilet soap, and rubber goods. In Berlin, absolutely everybody 'deals' – I was there recently, and saw it. The ladies of noble Prussian families are busy transacting business, and so are waitresses, drugstore clerks, high-school students.... I was laughed at, and it was considered quite unconscionable that I should sit on my haunches in the valleys of Chiemgau with the present and future well-being of a family to think of, and neglect my 'opportunities'.

This is Germany today. True, southern Germany has remained sceptical about all the Prussian noise in victory, and thus has kept cleaner. The great majority of the workers and practically all the intellectuals are bitter opponents of the regime. And the farmers remain wedded to their old, unchangeable patterns of thinking and living, shrug their shoulders over the triumphs, and cannot be brought to 'participate'.

But what good does it do? Industry pulls the strings; it has controlled the General Staff since the days of Ludendorff. The instrument of power is terror, and the industrialists hold tight to it. They control every means of influencing public opinion, and have thereby stupefied the great unproductive mass – salaried people, office workers, most of the lower ranking government employees – to the point of idiocy. The rest is a mixture of business people and nobility come down in the world, melted into a middle-class lump with the newly created officers and quick-turnover fellows. These people are more materialistic than the Bolshevik Russians, live from day to day, and haven't the slightest conception of the grim little game that has been begun here.

A certain quotation has remained in my mind since the end of the First World War.... It is a quotation which provides me with a certain bitter hope, albeit for motives that are not in the least proletarian. It is a quotation from Balzac's *César Birotteau*: 'Et *c'est la bourgeoisie elle-même, qui écoutera chanter sa* Noce du Figaro.'

And it should be observed that Balzac's viewpoint was that of a conservative, as is my own, and further observed that between this viewpoint and that of the nationalists is a chasm as wide as a canyon. To be a conservative means to believe in the immutable laws of this old earth: this earth that will begin to shake and quake when the day comes to cleanse itself of all this filth.

And this is where the crack begins which runs through my heart – which runs through the heart of every man for whom Germany is not identical with the Deutsche Bank or the German Steel Association. The poor little remnant of the German intelligentsia is also supposed to become part of the amorphous and comfortable docile mass of vegetable pedlars. For the 'good of the nation', I am expected to become 'adjusted'. Specifically, I am required to deify this Reich, and the gentleman from the furnished room who has made himself its leader. I am supposed to sing in praise of deceit, of murder, of treaty-breaking. And I am supposed to join in the shrieks, the jubilant shouts as the enemy falls like a torch from his exploding aeroplane.

Yes, and this is truly effrontery enough to take the breath away, they are now demanding that a man forget everything he has learned in the course of travel and conversation abroad, and adopt comments about other countries of the Propaganda Ministry – a ministry of salesmen turned diplomats, informed by teachers turned foreign correspondents! To resolve my differences with God, I am supposed to adopt the thoroughly base and Godless contention that right is what is useful for Germany! I, who believe I know something about the laws of history and geopolitics, am expected to lower myself to the level of the canaille and scum of this nation, and believe in the permanence of a regime whose Magna Carta was a broken treaty and whose foundations are largely propaganda!

In a Berlin movie theatre recently, I saw the newsreel in which Hitler, standing in front of the historic railway car in the Forest of Compiègne, receives the news of the capitulation of France; and then begins to dance on one foot like an Indian; a dirty old pig playing at being a boy, less worthy of respect than the banned Kaiser, who is still paying for his sins.

Among these sins I count such actions as conducting the orchestra of the Potsdam Life Guards, and with old Franz Josef present, slapping King Ferdinand of Bulgaria on his blue-uniformed backside as the latter was bending over a map.

Nevertheless, I still remember the cold March morning when one of our farmhands came back from town with the news that the old Kaiser had died. Monarchs have an importance in the scheme of things. They carry the dignity of the people they rule like a cloak around their shoulders. The life of that simple farmhand was ennobled by being the true servant to a true master, and I have been brought up in the same tradition of duty and obedience. But I have never been so ashamed of my countrymen as I was there in that movie house, surrounded by the clamour of a mob in ecstasy over the sight of its hopping Führer. I stood up and left. The gesture was understood, and nasty remarks came from left and right; I was supposed to do that hopping filth the honour of applauding it. If I had given any clearer expression to what I was really thinking, I would very likely have been lynched.

Oh, and the day in July when out of the loudspeaker in the square of Rosenheim, into the burning hot afternoon came Hitler's triumphal speech about his 'last peace proposal to England' – this, too, I shall never forget. The atmosphere was suffocatingly close, filled as it was with the greed and inordinate desires of people gone berserk with success. Old fogies, threatening that, 'We'll take up England with a vacuum cleaner.' And the big-talking rear-echelon warrior, home from the wars for the moment with the inevitable office chippy on his arm, and in line with his role here of strategic expert, announcing that 'England will take fourteen days, at most.'

Hemmed in as I was by spiritually sick people, I knew that a terrible presence was already beginning to move about in that stifling night. Knowing as I did that England's answer must inevitably be 'No', I felt more alone among these thousands of people than if I had been at the North Pole.

As I write now, knowing full well what the end must be, I can well imagine the first day of a future occupation of Germany by English troops, when an English sergeant, simply because he has nothing better to do, puts a few bullets into me: I can well imagine that victory by the others will be followed by political blunders. I am far from making the mistake of thinking that nothing but devils live here, while nothing but angels live over there. Nevertheless, I cannot overlook the fact that a European psychosis is nearing its end in the dance of death that is going on in Germany, the psychosis of nationalism, and that Europe must now decide either to destroy it, or be itself destroyed.

Why must I honour as a force, foreseen at the time of the creation of the world, an idea – nationalism – which the builders of the cathedrals in Germany's greatest period had never heard of, which, indeed, never existed before 1789 and which the Nazis, who otherwise pose as the great liquidators of the French Revolution, have 'recreated' out of dusty old scrolls?

Why must I equate with basic human feelings like love and hate a philosophy which puts an aura of heroism around mercantilism and the bourgeois drive for power, and which is today as rancid and flat as the whole of Rousseau. Nationalism is as tattered and dust-covered as the banner of Girondism itself, which great Carlyle called the worst of all time. It was possible only at a time of generalised atheism, and purposelessness, and brute force. Of course, I.G. Farben welcomed Hitler – he provided their poison factory with the aura of a philosophy!

The businessmen from the Ruhr were well aware of what they were doing when they hired this sombre bandit. But should I pretend that I feel myself closer to a German coachman than to the French historian with whom I have been corresponding for decades, to keep this mercantilist ideology from going entirely to shreds? Am I supposed to make no protest when this same nationalism, supposedly the specially ordained protector of all the chief treasures of our national heritage, then turns about and grossly, cynically toys with these as only a barbarian would do?

What price a forest if the 'national' interest calls for a cellulose factory? Or a German cathedral that stands in the way of an autobahn? What is the value of a tiny remnant of the German soul when aggression is in the works and an entire nation is being systematically turned into cavemen – when their spiritual centre is to be destroyed, and they are to be turned into an amorphous mass, whose only form is formlessness itself?

But we must be completely clear: Why, if nationalism really is one of the basic impelling forces of mankind, as its apologists contend, was it discovered in such comparatively recent times as the French Revolution? How is it that this 'basic force' did not exist in the days of the *Song of the Nibelungs*? And how does one explain the fact that in 1400 there was a German nation, but no nationalism – while today, when nationalism is in full bloom, even Goebbels gags a little at the statement that this conglomeration of wage earners, sergeants-gone-berserk, and virgin-typists is a nation? If nationalism is truly the hallmark of a people in the prime of its youth and energies, how does it happen that under its aegis morality decays, ancient customs die out – that men are uprooted, the steadfast derided, the thoughtful branded, the rivers poisoned, and the forests destroyed?

Why, if this is a high watermark in our national life, has our speech been vulgarised in this unprecedented way? Why is there such a worsening of all social forms? How have we come to this reneging on treaties and our given word? And how did we arrive at this pimp's German, with all foreign words fearfully excised, which is today written and spoken by all of German officialdom, from the General Staff down to the 'war commentators'?

Try, if you can, in these, our 'great' days, to build a cathedral; at the end, you will have a blasphemy in stone. Listen to a lady on the radio read a German fairy tale, and you will begin to feel you are in a bordello. Mouth the names of the men into whose hands the nation has been delivered: Dwinger, and Steguweit, and Thorak, and Speer, and Herms Niel; then just speak the word 'Germany', and the lie of the combination will make you choke. Place yourself amongst the crowd as it is roaring out one of Haydn's songs, and you will think you are listening to a beer-garden concert, with all the usual noise, and behind, the usual smell from the men's room…. And this is nationalism? – this thing that Frederick of Prussia knew nothing about when that chief Machiavellian of his time drew his dagger in an attempt to turn failure into success amidst the ruins of his life?

But the time is 1940, and not 1848. We do not think of St Paul's Church when asked to associate with the word 'Germany'; we at once think of 'Deutsche Bank' and 'German Steel Association'. Therefore, let us put the following problem in arithmetic to the nationalists:

Your up-to-date man, who prides himself on his knowledge of

technocracy, will certainly agree that the geopolitical importance of a particular country can be measured by the time it takes to cross it. But new techniques are constantly being used in transportation, and from year to year the time it takes to cross a particular country is lessened. Once, it took twenty-four hours to go from Memel to Lindau. Today, it takes only two. Thus technology has reduced the geopolitical importance of Germany to something comparable, let us say, to that of the one-time Grand Duchy of Saxe-Weimar. And yet, hardheaded realism and materialism are to be laid aside while I view this same geopolitical atom with the same awe and wonder as did the princely Electors being carried to Frankfurt behind a creaking span of oxen! Technology, which is supposedly so logical, thus becomes inconsistent in its very own area!

Is such a symbiosis of technology and autarchy even possible? Doesn't technology itself mix different peoples, and standardise their tastes and requirements? What is the point of building an auto to go two hundred kilometres an hour when after an hour's drive you come to a border post, where a full-bearded Teuton waggles a threatening finger as he forbids further travel as 'contrary to the interests of the government'?

I will be glad when the day comes that technology is sent to the Devil, like all the other overrated ideas of mankind. I see a time coming when science, if it does not actually disappear, will be relegated to the periphery of our way of life, and mankind will have a totally different central interest. But because science is now so important, those in control think that this perverse condition can be maintained indefinitely. For example, one region has a surplus of lemons, and another does not have enough. Powerful means of transportation are constantly running back and forth between the two regions – and yet no lemons can be carried from one to the other. If this kind of thing can really be enforced indefinitely, what other purpose can technology serve than filling all life with stench, noise, filth, and the roar of the degenerate masses?

Nationalism, no matter how loudly defended today, is almost finished, and the coup de grace will come in this most mob-like of all wars. Tomorrow it will be behind us, an ugly, sweaty dream. The idea of a united Europe was not always upheld by me, but I know now that we can no longer afford the luxury of considering it a mere idea. Europe must either make any further wars impossible, or this cradle of great ideas will see its cathedrals pulverised, and its landscape turned into a plain.

Today, on the way home from Villach, I stopped at the quarry, shimmering under the autumn sun. A sand viper, about to take its midday siesta, was just crawling into the protecting shadow of the rocks. I looked at it for a long time, and the brightly coloured reptile looked back at me out of its knowledgeable and weird and mutely mournful eyes. There is a legend at home that these reptiles were created out of the old and ever renewed earth to suck up all the acids and poisons which ooze out of the deeds resulting from human cruelty, and out of all our sins.

For a long time I remained there, watching. Then I walked the rest of the way back to the lake. The sun was setting behind the mountains, and I felt the cold breath of autumn; felt, also, sadness for another year almost gone, and for all of the life out of which we are being cheated because Herr Krupp wants more money and the generals cannot stop their self-aggrandisement.

Nor has this quiet valley escaped their noisy attentions: in the street below, a company of soldiers marches by, under the command of a lieutenant sitting on a brindled mare like a dog on top of a picket fence. They are singing some new marching song introduced by the Nazis. The old soldiers' songs have been discarded as 'sentimental' – and the new ones have the thin, overworked sound of something heard from a bar-room.

But on the local billboard where yesterday the conscientious head of the local Nazis had painted 'God Punish England' amidst all the other greatly oversized slogans, there was today something else. An inconceivable, an almost godless thing had happened, and I was perhaps the first to come upon it. There, where 'God Punish England' had been inscribed in letters of fire across the billboard, someone had erased 'England' and had put in its place the name of a geographical region far from this outermost region of the one-time Holy Roman Empire. The wrath of God had been invoked to fall down upon – *Prussia*.

9 November 1940

Dr Strauss is an Armed Forces psychologist, and passes on the mental condition of prospective officer candidates. He told me that one young man, asked about his feelings and the impression made upon him by his reading of *Faust*, replied: 'Well, that Faust was certainly quite a boy. But you know, Doctor, that thing with Gretchen, he probably shouldn't have done that.'

So much for the legacy left to his people by great Goethe.

The twenty-second anniversary of the 1918 Munich Revolt had just passed, and we talked about it. As a Royalist, I had opposed it. All the old pictures rose up in my mind: the artillery unit from the Rhineland sent to put down the uprising, which camped the evening before the King's abdication almost in front of the windows of my place in Pasing, and which was immediately disarmed ... the emaciated nags, torn horse collars, hungry cannoneers.... And the rattle of the machine guns, and the dead lying on the much-trodden ground, so tiny and flat against it that they seemed already part of the earth....

Then the triumphal parade of the newly born republic! Ingenuous, middle-class, as only that dear old Munich could be! Bearers of red flags who had obtained their banners only after hurrying about days earlier to get the required procurement orders; behind them, veterans of many a Socialist battle at the polls, little, bent gentlemen in spotted tailcoats.... Oh, I remember that this parade of the protesting masses even included several frightful, camel's-hair top hats waggling in the crowd, old-fashioned and thin as sawn-off stovepipes, towering over the Revolution.

Then, standing on buckboards, a couple of excited old fogies beating away with hammers at the brightly painted metal of the court purveyors' shields, and finally a completely unforgettable scene: on one of the strange stone animals in the Lenbach Fountain, old Mühsam, looking not too unlike a winged Assyrian ox with his berry-brown beard, holding forth rapturously to an enraptured throng....

That was the revolution in Munich.

In Munich, just after the turn of the century, it was the custom for officials charged with the issuance of driving permits to appear for the tests wearing top hats. I can remember that on the second day of the Revolution, in the midst of a mass uprising which proclaimed to the world its determination to topple all crowned heads into the dust, there suddenly came a vast and jubilant roar from the great crowd at the Karlsplatz: somehow, the rumour had spread that King Ludwig was coming – *King Ludwig*, who had drowned thirty years before in Lake Starnberg, but who never died in the imagination of his subjects – King Ludwig, who built castles and ruined himself for Richard Wagner, who drove across the mountains in deep snow in an eight-horse sleigh seated behind powdered, periwigged lackeys.

But this is Munich: infinitely unpolitical, possessed of a baroque little gambler's soul that the Prussians will never understand – Berlin's natural opposite.

The Nazis, with their imbecile technocratic goals, will never remake Bavaria in their image, even if their occupation lasts another ten years. And even if they were to win the war, they would still fail, for the following reasons: (a) they lack souls; and (b) they lack humour. As the enemies of the laughter of men, they are more afraid of humour than of a new declaration of war.

To come back to Munich: I was there recently, and the hotel was unheated, the service poor, and the linen of doubtful cleanliness. The restaurants are open at certain hours only, and the moment the doors are opened a hungry, hysterical mob streams into the dining-room. Elbows in the neighbour's ribs, this horde flies off to the nearest empty table, and crouches there, eyes bloodshot, teeth bared, until a bowl in which a paper-thin slice of some strange meat is swimming in an even stranger kind of gravy is brought to them. The whole thing has the look of the zoo when the keepers begin their regular feeding of the apes.

But this is not the main thing that will remain in my mind from this latest visit to the once elegant city the Prussians have ruined. Near the main station, a long line of people wound down Senefelderstrasse, that hideous and endlessly dismal thoroughfare. When I asked someone what the line was for, I was told that these people were waiting to get into a bordello – in broad daylight, in a queue that stretched to the station square and blocked traffic – soldiers on leave, war workers, and even a few women. (The women were there certainly by error and out of a herd instinct, had no idea of the purpose of the line, and were the subject of the cynical, half-audible jokes and nasty laughter of the men.) I learned that this day's business was about what it usually is, but that when there were trains crowded with soldiers on leave, the police had to be called. At such times, the line might be limited to a hundred at a time, and maids employed by families in the area might be called in to 'help out'.

Really, this is the kind of thing that goes on in Munich today. This discreet establishment belongs to the same Christian Weber who was a busboy at the Blue Boar Café before he became Herr Hitler's pet, and able to criticise an artist like Clemens von Franckenstein, and live in the papal chambers of the old Royal Residence. Munich's sense of humour found expression recently when a whole flock of new field-marshals and other new demigods were created by the regime. To satisfy Göring and his insatiable hunger for titles, the position of World Marshal was created, according to the joke; Goebbels, in view of his gay temperament, was named Half-World Marshal; but Christian Weber received the title of Senefeld Marshal.

The title, of course, has reference to this discreetly flourishing establishment, which brings in handsome sums to the Great Man's dinner companion, and is, as I have said, on Senefelderstrasse.

June 1941

I have a tenuous contact with the German Embassy in Moscow, and I knew, therefore, what had to come – and what now has come.[52]

The horrible part of it is, that these people are so lost in their own inner darkness that they did not even realise what was happening. They persisted in deluding themselves with: 'And now he is negotiating with Russia.' And their eyes, big enough for the digestion of half the world, glittered even more greedily than usual. 'Russia is going to let us march across its territory to get to India! German divisions are already in the Caucasus!' This, at a time when grim, dark, smoke-filled clouds were already blotting out the sun in the East!

'Tomorrow we'll be in India.' And Obersturmbannführer Semmelbei thinks of himself as Viceroy over the Indians, in place of some haughty British aristocrat. Hatred of England is something that dates from the Boer War of 1899. It has a specifically mob character, and is the dominant emotion of the German masses at the moment. It is essentially a hatred of an oligarchy – the German elementary schoolteachers who manipulate public opinion feel insulted at the very existence of a clearly defined society of classes anywhere in the world. For example, one of their badly paid foreign correspondents, Frau Irene Seligo of the *Frankfurter Zeitung*, has never been able to forgive England for not according her the treatment ordinarily given an ambassador, and immediately on her arrival, whisking her off to Buckingham Palace for a reception by the King and Queen.

Underneath, there is the rumbling of all the various little hidden desires. One wants to emigrate, and has his eye on an English coffee plantation. Another wants to get hold of English cloth and English tobacco to be sent home. And our 'experienced secretary', now the typical example of German womanhood, hopes that her fiancé in the SS will ship home the Chippendale pieces she requires to complete her four-room dream apartment.

Kostja Leuchtenberg informs me that the Nazis have completed their 'economic planning' insofar as overseas posts are concerned, and that all the openings in Nigeria, Kenya, or South-West Africa have been filled by German engineers.

Recently, I saw Jannings' film, *Ohm Krüger*. The audience was not moved by scenes representing the camp for women prisoners, nor by the cruelties which were supposedly perpetrated on the Boer women. No, the clamour came in a court scene when an English aristocrat wearing the Order of the Garter was shown going to an audience with Queen Victoria! ... the hatred of the termite heap for everything not yet reduced to the size of a termite. A termite heap, this is what the industrialisation of Germany has brought about, this is what the sociological ideal of the Messrs. Krupp, Thyssen, Röchling, and Hösch amounts to.

Oh, there are still a few people who have not been absorbed into the heap. There are the intellectuals, once the best part of Germany and now barely three per cent of the population. There are the farmers, a sociological anchor to windward in any epoch, who have not let themselves be fooled, no matter what the propaganda, and who know that they are threatened by the 'industrial penetration of the flatlands' advocated by Herr Röchling. There is also Bavaria, once considered the Cradle of the Movement, which long since put a fence between it and Nazism, and now hold itself as much apart as the Vendée during the French Revolution.

Towards the end of March, as German tank columns were rolling south-west down the wide Wiener Chaussee highway on their way to 'punish Serbia' by throttling a little country, I saw an old farmer standing at the side of the road. Each time a tank rumbled by, the old man spat forcefully. When Hess flew to England, there was widespread rejoicing among the villagers because, as they said, 'the Crown Prince got out,' signifying that he had left because he knew the game was up, and was getting out while he could.

But these elements, the intellectuals, the farmers, and the Bavarians are, of course, all that has survived of the Old Germany. The majority, that vast termite heap, was dreaming about a bargain between Germany and Russia at a time when the first shots were already being fired in the East. Nobody here had any idea of the real situation. Never did a people tumble more helplessly, more stupidly into catastrophe!

And never was a people so badly, so irresponsibly led! Schulenburg,[53] highly esteemed as a gentleman of the old school in Moscow, tried last winter after Molotov's trip to Berlin to warn against an attack, but Hitler would not even receive him. Köstring, the military attaché, was roared at by Hitler, and called a Russophile because he pleaded the urgent necessity of correctly assessing the Red Army. The barometer obstinately refused to register 'clear and fine' – so they smashed it.

I can remember as a boy listening to discussions of General Staff officers who came to our house. With what care these men of the old von Moltke school approached the problem called Russia! But the General Staff men of today were trained in Ludendorff's school. They are still planning in terms of the First World War. With the arrogance of their dead mentor, they are counting on a *promenade militaire*.

And the German industrialists are planning to swamp Russia with cheap radios and consumer goods! The Russian people are to be bribed with the promise of electrification and cheap, mass-produced consumer goods. The man of the vast stretches of the Volga steppes, this enigma, who will always be completely beyond the understanding of a West German – who specifically wants his own Russian system and who, above all, wants 'not to become like the West' – this man is now equated to a German by our brilliant businessmen!

This stupid, arrogant view of the Russians as Hottentots to be bribed with trinkets and cast-off top hats is the first basic mistake. The second is the incredible underestimation of the distances involved. At the time of my visit to Russia ten years ago there were villages in the northern Urals and the Pechora River Basin which had still – fourteen years after the November Revolution – not heard of the fall of the Czar, in fact, did not even know that there had been a world war.

But worst of all is the underestimation of the strange Slavic soul, only now beginning to be awakened, still haunted by awful nightmares. Never will I forget the comment made in St Petersburg in 1912 by a Russian farmer newly come to town on seeing an aeroplane take off for the first time in his life: 'Most likely, he gets thirty roubles a month, at most thirty-five. Thirty-five roubles a month, and for that *he dares deny God!*'

German technocrats who put this utterance down as belonging to a primitive do not understand. But they will meet this peasant in the vast Hyperborean stretches of Russia, and then they will find what was not dreamed of in their philosophy; the demon world of a people which is really 'young', not as a phrase in propaganda, but which has not, despite everything, let go of its gods.

I talked about this last Easter Sunday with Kostja Leuchtenberg, who came back from the Rand mines two years ago, and who, as a native Russian, knows that world as he knows the West. He agreed that with this war we come at last to that moment in history when for the first time the Slavic world directly confronts the Western. Despite the constant talk here, through Hitler's mouth, of 'Destiny' and the 'All-powerful', this Germany is as cynical as only an ageing Western nation can be. Russia, on the other hand, which twenty-four years ago took up its Cross and for the sake of distant goals has suffered, frozen, and gone hungry, is like that blasphemer I described earlier who in Dostoyevsky's words is closer to God than the sceptic.

Yesterday, at the dawn of a burning-hot day, I turned the knob on my radio and to my surprise heard Herr Goebbels declaring war on yesterday's allies. I turned away, deeply affected. It is entirely possible that the war now beginning will engulf me, my worldly goods, my physical life, and my children as well. It is entirely possible, also, that I myself will be pulled by the eddies from this latest stroke of Hitler's genius, and dragged down.

Nevertheless, my first reaction was wild jubilation. I have never ceased to believe in the core of this people, deep as this has been hidden away, by now scarcely discernible. This nation is about to take a great and salutary reducing course which will free it of its ugliness, and teach it, at a cost of what may well be immense suffering, to believe in other gods than the unholy Trinity of Krupp, Röchling, and the cheap radio.

In their immense vanity, Satan's own have overreached themselves, and now they are in the net, and they will never free themselves again. That is the fact, and this it is that rejoices my heart. I hate you. I hate you waking and sleeping; I hate you for undoing men's souls, and for spoiling their lives; I hate you as the sworn enemy of the laughter of men.... Oh, it is God's deadly enemy which I see, and hate, in you.

In every one of your speeches you make a mockery of the Spirit, which you have silenced, and you forget that the private thought, the thought born in sorrow and loneliness, can be more deadly than all your implements of torture. You threaten all who oppose you with death, but you forget: our hatred is a deadly poison. It will creep into your blood, and we will die shouting with joy when our hate pulls you down with us into the depths.

Let my life be fulfilled in this way, and let my death come when this task is completed! This promise has come out of the heart of the people you are now striking, and I set it down, at this moment, since it applies to you as well as to us:

If you banish God from the earth, we will meet him under the earth. And then we, the underground men, will sing a song to God, who is Joy....

September 1941

Recently, at the little station of Garching, in Upper Bavaria, I saw the first trainload of Russian prisoners of war.

I should say: I did not see them. I smelled them. A line of sealed freight cars was standing on a spur, and the summer breeze carried over to me a foul stench of urine and human excrement. When I went closer I saw the urine and excrement seeping through the floorboards and cracks in the cars and down onto the tracks. 'They are packed in there like cattle.' The militiaman who said this to me did not seem to agree at all with this treatment of defenceless men – he seemed, in fact, truly disturbed. 'They are so starved in the prison camps that they tear the grass out of the ground and swallow it.'

Here is something that happened locally. The son of a poverty-stricken peasant family returned home recently from America following an adventure-filled odyssey. His mother and father, poor as beggars but of excellent repute, welcomed their son home with open arms and a great dinner, and the prodigal ate and drank and went to bed. But during the evening, he had exhibited several hundred-dollar bills. The parents debated the matter for a long time while the son slept. Then, unity having been established, the mother got a long kitchen knife and slit open her son's throat for the sake of the money: honest people, otherwise, upright people....

Yet when I voice a long-held theory of mine, that behind all this horror and this unprecedented denial by a basically well-meaning people of all decency – that behind it, there lies concealed a cosmic process, a gigantic psychosis and the unleashing of a horde of demons, I am laughed at. I am called a fabricator of nightmares, and am told that a certain amount of physiological coarsening is always observable in people during wartime. It will turn out that I was right in the end, even if it takes decades.

And now it begins to appear that the theory must be widened. The death of the few good people who remain must also be included among the symptoms of the disease, as though these deaths were part of the plan, according to some frightful logic. Clemens von Franckenstein became ill last winter, just before he was planning to visit me for a few days. The sickness appeared to be a severe grippe, and was treated as such. But he did not improve and had to be removed to a hospital.

Recently, I visited him there, and was terrified at the way his face had shrunk. And today, a friend of mine who is a doctor sent me a copy of a Munich medical weekly, in which lung-cancer case histories are given. The very first case, with the use of initials, an indiscretion which pained me very much, was that of Clé: that good and clean man. Clé, who in bearing and character has always appeared to me to be among the last true German noblemen!

The very same day, as though fate had really decided to take away all my friends, as though loneliness has become part of our martyrdom, I got word of the severe illness of Clé's cousin, Count Erwein Schönborn. Master of the great Wiesentheid estate, nephew of former Reich Chancellor Hohenlohe, a man of truly humanistic temper, he chose medicine over the usual career as diplomat or jurist. He became a doctor after the most comprehensive training in surgery. At home, after breakfast in a salon among tapestries woven by Raphael, it was the custom for this extremely wealthy aristocrat to leave his guests and get on his motorcycle for the morning calls on his patients – he accepted no fees. Now, this tremendous man of letters and friend of everything human appears to have fallen ill after years of doing too much.

We were, Franckenstein, he, and I, a little band of friends joined by certain sports and personal experiences, but above all by a common attitude towards life and by the hope that a better time might come. When I think that this man, too, on whom I counted so heavily to help shape the future of this nation, will soon be lost to me, I shudder.

In the theatre, the lights flicker and go out. The stage empties, and from somewhere behind it an icy wind sweeps down. Only the larvae are left in the orchestra seats. In deathly loneliness, before an audience of degenerates, the last scene must be played out.

Berlin, of course, is far from such melancholy thoughts! Berlin has the loud voice of the confident, it is riding the crest of a torrent of victories, it has the look of the fattest days of the Wilhelms. The deserving are parcelling out the goods of the earth, as thrown to them by Herr Hitler.... People transact 'business' breakfast extremely well in restaurants reserved for the demigods of this regime, and all in all have the pleased air of a man who has a birthday every day. On my last visit, I dined at the same place where the carryings-on of the scions of Prussian nobility so absorbed me several years ago. With me this time was Frau v. K., my dancing partner as a girl, who now at first sight somehow reminded me of an oaken dining-room buffet. The lady had a huge bosom, and that prosperous-looking physiognomy so often found among ladies of her class who have passed the forty mark.

This sylph of yesteryear produced out of her handbag and dangled before my nose a pair of handsome bronze candlesticks – the *hors d'oeuvres*. According to the testimony, also produced, these candlesticks had once served to light the desk of Napoleon at Saint-Cloud, long since destroyed by fire....

Robbed, naturally – but this is war, isn't it? When I tried to say that I did not want what was to me stolen goods, and refused them on the basis of my insufficient means, I was given a lecture on economics by the lady. I learned all about how happy the banks were to lend money, how paper money automatically depreciated in value, and why I, as a father of two, should certainly be able to seize opportunity by the forelock when it arose. After the candle-sticks came an offer of French cognac, of Parisian lingerie, and finally of a breeding pair of Sealyham terriers that a friend of Frau v. K.'s with an estate near Rennes had 'secured' – these last, obvi-ously, could not be carried in one's handbag like candlesticks for on-the-spot appraisal.

However, when I refused all these offers, the temperature fell sharply, and Madame took her leave, having decided she had become involved with an idiot. The movement of her yardwide backside conveyed her deep contempt.

Paul Wiegler, the last man remaining at the former Ullstein publishing house on Kochstrasse who also worked for the Ullsteins, told me about the old doorkeeper there. This man still, somehow, is in touch with his former employers in New York, and according to information he has received, one of the brothers, a former multi-millionaire, is close to going hungry in his old age. I knew none of these unapproachable Ullstein brothers, but now and then I saw something of their ant-like industry and their puritanical rules of conduct. Now they are poverty-stricken. They might be interested to know that an official government agency has been set up, complete with telephone, card files, and secretary, which calls itself the Reich Office for Ethics in Business Operations.[54]

I used this opportunity to call upon Princess Friedrich Leopold, a close friend of my wife's parents. The Princess is the sister of the deceased Empress, sister-in-law of that Kaiser who, with his wife, left the country 'by public request', so to speak, and daughter-in-law of Prince Friedrich Karl, who was in command at Mars-la-Tour. She is alert and quite agile despite her eighty years, and in no respect reminds one of her royal sister. Possessed of a mind free of prejudices and in excellent health, she bicycles from Glienicke when she visits my in-laws at Strausberg, a trip across the whole mammoth city, and is not at all inclined to be gentle when she talks about her imperial brother-in-law and his demeanour as Emperor.

Of course, she has hardly anything left of the brilliance that was Glienicke in her father-in-law's time. Most of the castle has been sold, and her capital has shrunk to almost nothing in truly tragic fashion. Of her three sons, one fell in the first days of the last war, the second died in an accident during a riding competition, and the last of her sons, now doubly dear as a result, has given her great sorrow because of certain unfortunate inclinations. With their marvellous nose for such things, the Nazis got wind of these aberrant inclinations shortly after they got into power, and have been blackmailing the mother ever since. Periodically, they jail the prince, and demand an appropriate ransom. He is freed for a few weeks, and then rearrested. And the game begins again. When the Princess sought help from Herr Göring, he kept her waiting for two hours in an ante-room full of typists and SS louts. After the two-hour wait, the Royal Prussian Infantry Captain (retired) and model of a modern field marshal finally appeared, his hands in his pockets, chomping the inevitable cigar, and greeted the daughter-in-law of the victorious general at Metz as follows:

'What is it you wanted?'

This is Herr Göring, champion of the modern version of *enrichez-vous*, and as such, the ideal and white hope of the German bourgeoisie.

We talked a great deal about the dead Kaiser, whose reaction on learning of the death in action of her eldest son the Princess cannot forget. Wilhelm II was obligated to take some note of the death. To console the grieving parents he therefore sent a telegram, as follows: '*Noblesse oblige.*' This was the entire text.

I admit that I have come with the passage of time to think in more kindly fashion about the forgotten and deserted Kaiser. It seems to me that with his exile in Doorn he paid for his sins. I only saw him once, when he was 'on duty', had been angered by some military detail or other, and began to shout more loudly and shake his rather fat and short-fingered hand more violently than befits a king. The Hohenzollern decorations which later were contemplated as overtures in view of my monarchical leanings turned, amusingly enough, into a wooden souvenir from Doorn, carved by His Majesty's own two hands, when it was found out that my duty lay not to the House of Prussia, but to the House of Wittelsbach.

If, nevertheless, I have more to say about the dead monarch than the average German, this is because there was always a connection between my social class and the Court. The links were those old men, Deputies and holders of offices at Court, who were completely informed about all internal matters and gladly passed on full details during the course of hunt dinners in Masuria. People in our circle thus knew about the Krupp and Eulenberg Circle scandals five years before the press did, and I can remember one truly Hamlet-like episode which took place behind the scenes in Wilhelm's Germany during 1896 or 1897....

My Uncle Marcell, who was attached to the German Embassy in St Petersburg, was constantly travelling back and forth between that city and Berlin, and so he was glad to make use of my parents' estate as a place to rest between trips. The result was that we knew everything that happened in Berlin, as reflected in the gossip of the Czar's court, in the shortest possible time. I can remember a July morning after breakfast when I had gone to read the newspaper in my father's study, while the two old gentlemen, my uncle and my father, remained sitting at the table in the dining-room adjoining.

I should explain that at that time the newspapers had reported that the Emperor had narrowly escaped serious injury aboard the *Hohenzollern* when a smoke sail fell off the mast and hit him in the eye as he was promenading on deck. The wound was light, but rather painful, the newspapers reported, and there was a further notice that the officer of the watch responsible for the accident, a Lieutenant von Hahncke, died in the course of an outing several days after this Lilliputian catastrophe, and that his corpse and bicycle were pulled from the bottom of a waterfall in Norway.

Now, listening to my uncle, I learned what no newspaper had reported, what had taken place backstage. Lieutenant von

Hahncke was a passionate bicyclist – this was the heyday of the sport. He had ridden his bicycle around the deck of the *Hohenzollern* a number of times when the Kaiser, who hated the new sport, was also there. Wilhelm had him confined to quarters and thenceforth felt a certain animosity towards him. It was the purest bad luck that Hahncke had the watch when the smoke sail fell and hit the Kaiser as he was on deck.

But now something inconceivable occurred, something that made the blood of a twelve-year-old boy hearing about it turn cold. The Kaiser ordered the entire watch assembled on deck, and then, wild with rage, struck Hahncke in the face – and Hahncke, struck thus before all these fellow officers, also forgot himself and remembering only what is basic to all of us, *hit him back.*

Dead silence. All present merely stared. Then, Hahncke turned and went below. A day later, following the ship's arrival in Norway, the Lieutenant asked for and was quickly granted shore leave. That evening the officer and his bicycle were taken from the waterfall. He had, of course, committed suicide – there was no question of murder. He had killed himself in payment for his insult to his king. This was confirmed to me by relatives of the dead man twenty-two years later.

Still, it would be unfair to judge the Kaiser on the basis of a single incident arising out of his lack of self-control. In private, he was a well-meaning though basically deeply insecure man. But as soon as he was called upon to appear in public, a kind of frenzy took hold of him, and to overcome this insecurity and appear in his own eyes a personage who 'knew how to take care of himself' he adopted a manner which was meant to show what a grim and unyielding military man he really was.

A friend of mine had the grim experience of watching this transformation take place before his eyes. He was host to the Kaiser during Army manoeuvres, and the Emperor had walked about the estate, talked pleasantly, and been altogether natural and charming. But then the manoeuvres began again, his adjutants appeared, and the Emperor was suddenly converted into the cranky, loud-voiced 'Imperator' the world knew; irritable, with an effect that was painful in every way.

At the same time, the tragicomedy was that this master of military nicety and the theatrical effect in uniforms was himself never quite able to appear correctly dressed. There was always something about his waist belt, his sword knot, or some other detail of uniform that was 'not quite'. An English naval officer told me that the Kaiser, who was among other things an admiral in the British Navy, once suddenly had the idea of 'inspecting' a British Mediterranean squadron at that moment involved in firing practice and totally unprepared for the visits of royalty. The officer described how Wilhelm II climbed the gangway of the flagship wearing a glittering admiral's uniform and – to the amusement of all – highly inappropriate white summer shoes.

At the very beginning of his exile, when the Emperor was still living at Amerongen, an English lady saw him at the wedding of some high-ranking couple of the Dutch nobility. The Kaiser was standing at the altar wearing his impressive general's uniform, complete with the Cord of the Black Eagle – and on his feet were those hideous leather leggings popularly called 'tootsie rolls' in my Army days. Recently, I saw one of the last photographs of the Kaiser, taken by my wife's uncle, who for ten years was Marshal of Nobility at Doorn. The photo shows the Kaiser peaceably sitting on a park bench, attired in a handsome soft suit, his hands clasped over the handle of a cane, feet comfortably crossed – every inch the dignified old gentleman. The only trouble was that on his feet the warm boots he was wearing were not buttoned correctly – so much so, that there was really no overlooking the fact.

I do not at all say that such things were offensive – rather, that they were comical and made one feel that a kind of irony was involved; as though an invisible hand were setting the balance right in this way for his compulsive exactitude in just such matters, and with a certain bonhomie reminding him of the tragicomedy in all human endeavour – 'See here, Kaiser, you are supposed to be the expert in precisely these matters; even you are far from perfect' – or something to that effect. I don't believe that accident is involved in such things. I believe that here we see the benevolent hand of God – when, in the midst of the most passionate lyrical or political effusion, crucial words become their ridiculous opposites by the printer's changing of a letter.

I do not believe in that famous 'extravagance' with which nature supposedly equipped him for his imperial role, as people used to say so often. I believe that only by the cruelest of ironies could this shy, insufficient, and basically deeply insecure man have been called to rule a Reich which has been drowned in trouble practically since the day it was founded: robber-barons' defeat in the Church-State battle, the von Arnim scandal, social crises, the deaths of two Kaisers.

I do not even hold him responsible for the dismissal of Bismarck, either alone or as the moving force. No serious student of history will blame Wilhelm for this. Was there actually room anymore for a conservative autocrat in a Germany which had industrialised itself overnight? Can one seriously imagine a symbiosis of Bismarck and I.G. Farben?

I believe that Germans generally are trying to appease their own bad consciences by shifting the blame to a single man. It was Germany itself which overnight tore itself loose from all its old ties, its ideals and its gods, and dismissed Bismarck from his functions that day in March. I believe that the Kaiser merely acted as the executive of the will of the people – and was himself the final expression of a time when almost every German was secretly a miniature Wilhelm II: just as progress-happy, just as loud, just as much adrift, torn loose from the old moorings. Just as provoking, just as tactless, just as much in love with himself as an irresistible force – and yet so insecure, so harmless, basically.

In 1905, I was at Torbole, on Lake Garda, when a convention of German druggists was held there. During the day, the delegates attended meetings, and at night they cruised the lake with their wives aboard chartered steamers. Their singing of *Still ruht der See* resounded across the lake – they were so sure of themselves, so certain that everyone about was as pleased by their activity as they themselves were. Suspended between dream and reality, they were really deeply to be pitied – symbols of a Germany basically quite harmless, but completely and entirely lost.

I am not, as I would imagine is obvious by now, an adherent or apologist for the House of Hohenzollern. I am not a gentleman of the bedchamber, nor am I inclined to Byzantinism. Nevertheless I believe that the way the sons of those singing pharmacists denied the Kaiser who was their own true representative during the days of catastrophe in 1918 was shameful.

In 1914, during those last days of July in Berlin, a crowd so huge I could not see to the end of it stood before the castle and chanted up to the Kaiser's windows....

'We want to see our Kaiser!'

'We want to see our dear Kaiser!'

This is what they chanted. They roared in tempo, and without ragged edges – as only a well-trained people who, at a moment's notice, can also organise their enthusiasm, can roar.

That was at the end of July, in 1914 – and yet, 220 weeks later, or 1,540 days, no impropriety was improper enough, no cynicism was cynical enough, to fling at him. This was after twenty-six years of his reign, more than enough time to make changes in leadership and come to know those areas in which he was insufficient. What did that gray-haired old man do in the 1,540 days following that chorus ending in curses and shame that was so much worse than he had done in the twenty-six previous years?

I know that the overthrow of the monarchy was inevitable, but I do believe that especially in a case like this, when an entire nation must also feel itself responsible, this should happen in a different way than it did. I do not believe that the Germans have a right to be ironic and superior, as the Goebbels press is in its articles about the Kaiser. Quite the contrary, I believe that there is every reason why the Germans should ponder their own sins and their own insufficiency – especially the General Staff, north German oligarchy, and the Prussian nobility.

Where was Ludendorff in his sovereign's hour of need? Where were these generals who, after Ludendorff, joined with the industrial oligarchy to drag this insufficient monarch into their bloody gamble? And where in that hour was that gray-haired Constable of the Throne of Prussia himself, Hindenburg, when his royal master, of whose weaknesses he was certainly well aware, needed help? He certainly could have done better than to wave his hand helplessly, and advise what was most comfortable for the generals: that Wilhelm kindly take himself off to another country.

It is easy to write, 'Loyalty is the mark of honour.' But it is not so easy to accept the fact that loyalty can be sworn to just once in a man's life; that once sworn to, it cannot be retracted the way one takes back an IOU that has been paid off; and that to be true until death is to take responsibility for one's life.

But this is precisely what the Swiss Guard did, when they defended with their lives, on 10 August 1792, the empty palace of a runaway king: they had taken an oath.

These victories in Russia may continue and history may even some day celebrate them as great and important (a thing I do not want to believe). Nevertheless, these generals, who only yesterday were so agitated over the wording of the oath of allegiance, and then turned about and swore to every possible thing that came into the minds of a gang of political criminals, will never be honoured as those Swiss farmers were. No one will ever place the marble figure of a wounded lion atop their graves.

Pain, and sorrow, and the unbearable shame in which we have been living these past eight years provide new perspectives. We are to be given a second chance. Once more, and for the last time, we are given the opportunity to look deep into ourselves and hold that private discourse which in 1918 in so cowardly a fashion we avoided doing.

'It is not, nor it cannot come to good,' as Hamlet says. He might have spoken for us, as well. No good can come of this cloud of victories, with the stink of crime, no good to a country whose foundations are propaganda and treason – no good to a people which pharisaically and self-righteously shifts the burden of its own sins onto its own ancient symbols, takes its oath to criminals, and is ready to take any oath and make any contract with Satan. No, the Devil's price merely goes up and up!

A storm is coming up over the heads of a people blindly drunk with victory, and the man who sees it is alone today in Germany. He is alone with his knowledge, and can see that the day is coming when he himself will have to make good on all large statements, spoken or written, that he has made. Of all the things that have ever been asked of life, just one remains: that in the hour of martyrdom, which our epoch requires of any man not part of the mass, a man be able to bring forth out of himself the strength that comes from having kept faith with the truth.

Surely, all human wishes, provided only that they are big enough, must come to fulfilment?

September 1941

This is how we live in Germany today....

Monday, a gigantic victory is announced. Tuesday, not a soul can remember what it was. Huge numbers of prisoners are reported captured; no one believes the figures. Day in and day out, trumpets on the radio announce more victories – and we switch off as soon as we hear the first notes of the fanfare, with a feeling of insult.

I don't know why it is that nothing remains in people's minds about these 'most gigantic pincer movements of all times' or of these trapped enemy armies many times bigger than at Sedan – or little more, anyway, than about the latest foot-and-mouth epidemic, or the fact that the ground frost is early this year – but so it is. Sometimes I think it is because of our general termite-heap condition, the termites being incapable of awareness of things outside the heap – I ponder this for a moment, and then I reject the idea. There is something else here, something more complex, something quite eerie, not quite to be put into words.

I do not know what it is, but I feel, as other people feel, that it is there and goes about in our midst, invisible –

If, despite my expectations, the facts really turn out to accord with the propaganda, I will nevertheless feel what I now do: these things are *beyond history*.

Another example of our living beyond history: Herr Bruno Brehm, who just a few years ago was a fixture in the ante-rooms of Jewish literati, writes gory dispatches from Lemberg about the corpses found there and supposed to be the work of the Cheka –

and blames it all on the Jews.[55] And so, without honour or truth or justice, we vegetate here. The lower classes, which we can say includes everybody but swastika-wearers, do not have enough food. The bureaucracy – former tailor's apprentices, bank trainees, and seminarians and theology students – calls for the hard life of the front line, and lives on 'diplomat' ration stamps, worth three times the ordinary food stamp.

Recently, when Herr Gauleiter Wagner honoured our little town with his presence, practically every chicken in the area was slaughtered to meet the needs of his entourage of drunkards and felons. Herr Hitler has his own private vegetable farm in Solln, near Munich, where SS guards patrol an electrically charged fence enclosing the hothouses of our vegetarian Tamerlane.

In the meantime the plebes are feeling the full fury of a German food industry gone chemical-crazy. Sugar is now made out of fir-wood pulp, sausage out of beech-wood pulp, and the beer is a stinking brew made of whey. Yeast is made out of a chemical, and marmalade is coloured to fool people into thinking it is the real thing. The same for butter, except that the colouring matter here also contains a vile and indigestible substance poisonous to the liver and doubtless responsible for the biliousness so common today. Everyone's eyes are yellow, and if I am to believe friends of mine who are doctors, the incidence of cancer has doubled in the last four years.

A true Prussian, an old hand at 'improvising' his life out of garbage cans, is in his glory when he can sweep away the natural abundance of Germany, which is more than enough to satisfy demand, and put in its place the substitute, the ersatz. Canned vegetables are also artificially coloured. The wine, except for what is guzzled by young officers, or black-marketed by Army paymasters, is unholy snake poison. The soap stinks as badly as 'New German' corruption, and the soles of the ski shoes I bought last winter after a series of battles over the ration coupon, turned into a sodden mess of cardboard after a half hour's walking. There is a story about a man who was clapped on the shoulder of his wood-synthetic suit by a friend, and absent-mindedly invited him to 'come in'.

The consequences of all this are already beginning to be apparent. As a result of the fermentation and gas resulting from pulpy, clayey bread, the air in the cafés is pestilential. No one even bothers anymore to hold back his wind. As a result of this systematic poisoning of the blood, people go about with boils and abscesses and their body liquids are fouled. The daily hunt for immediate necessities and envy of one's darling neighbours have combined to produce a nastiness, and a slackness in behaviour, such as would have been impossible even a short time ago.

A very chic and expensive sailing school, catering to the daughters of industrialists, is located on the lake nearby. Externally, it is a highly snobbish affair, but actually it is a little whorehouse, where the slim young things sleep with their bluff and rough and oh so marvellously brutal instructors. And in the café of the little village on the lake I heard the plump wife of Göring's personal physician give the details, in extenso, to her companion on exactly how the artificial insemination of Frau Göring had been achieved.

The absence of the men has led to grotesque situations. Since French prisoners of war are considered delectable, if forbidden fruit, it has happened in north Germany that a peasant woman will hide a Frenchman under her wheelbarrow load of potatoes and so smuggle him into her house.

In a village near here, the thirty-year-old straw-widow of a peasant off fighting in Russia strangled her two children by her 65-year-old father-in-law, on the moor. In my own basically highly moral little town, boulevard life has been introduced by north German females sent here by the Nazi 'Mother and Child' organisation; and the infection has spread to a portion of the native population. With the prisoner-of-war camp guards, the women have set up an 'Isle of Delight' here.

Recently, on my way to town I heard loud cries for help: What had happened was that one of these females had not paid attention to her three-year-old, and just while Madame was dallying with her lover, the child had fallen into the river and was drowned. I spent an hour trying to revive the infant, to no effect. The child was dead. The lady finally appeared, and although she played to the hilt the role of tragically bereft mother, that very evening I saw her promenading with her friend in front of the windows behind which her dead child was lying.

This was too much. That night, the village entertained the lady with a real cat's concert, ewers, fire horns, fire-fighting equipment. It was almost in the style of the old *Habern*, which up to fifty years ago ensured propriety in the villages in the simplest and most effective way possible, and which was unfortunately outlawed through the intervention of ignorant priests.

But now it begins to appear that a number of things which were supposed to have been finished are coming to life again, as such things do, on occasion: good and evil, the gods and the evil spirits of greed and bestiality. I do not know if the end of the world is at hand, as Dostoyevsky said. But this I do know, that these are years of a turning in human affairs which can never be changed again, and that the tyranny of an arrogant civilisation is at an end.

January 1942

This winter has fallen on us like an Apache. Apparently, the eternal sickening invocation of the Nordic which has gone on here these last years has been answered with this series of Hyperborean winters. For eight weeks now, like an image of the desolation which weighs down on this people's soul, whiteness has blanketed the contours of the earth. I have had to have a tunnel the height of a man dug from the house to the barns. Standing at the highest point of this Spitzbergian mass of ice, I am on a level with the second floor of the house.

Thus, for two months I have been as good as cut off from the world. To get a pound of meat is a two-hour journey on skis, it is a 24-hour, polar expedition to the nearest bank or to the dentist, and it takes two full days of travelling in a disgustingly filthy train, filled to the luggage racks with unclean and bad-smelling people, to get to Munich – a trip that used to take ninety minutes by car. This waste of time, inflicted on us by a regime which takes everything and gives nothing, means that you can do practically nothing involving the use of the mind. In the absence of all repairmen, a man has to become his own electrician, roofer, and plumber to thaw out frozen pipes and drains, and keep his household functioning.

Recently, on a walk through the frozen woods, I found a starving fawn that had been torn by a dog. I took it home, fatally wounded as it was, but it died in my arms – died with tears in its eyes, and a look of endless sadness, an indictment of the Creator for allowing one of His creatures to suffer so. Once, in the South

Atlantic, I saw a whaler in the process of killing a female accompanied by one of her offspring. The harpooner, a red-bearded
Irishman, kept putting harpoons into the whale. The intestines
were hanging out of the mangled body of the huge animal, and
nevertheless it continued to swim back and forth in the water
made red by its blood, trying with its shattered body to shield the
little whale. Since then, and the sight of that harpooner's freckled
face as he laughed derisively, and of that poor creature, faithful to
the end, I have believed in the existence of Satan as I believe in the
existence of God.

The winter has also changed the war. A spectre is rising out of
the snowy wastes of Russia, the spectre of retaliation, and my
honest countrymen are now trying to drown out their growing
fear by believing in miracles that will change everything. They
have hopes for gas which will destroy all life in a large country in
ten seconds, and a fantastic 'atom bomb', three of which would
suffice to sink the British Isles – yes, and an even more fantastic
tunnel, which is now supposedly being secretly dug under the
Channel from Calais, and out of which, one fine day, will come
strolling the German Army to cast all enemies of Brandenburg into
the dust.

In connection with this rumour about a Channel tunnel a rather
strange story was told me on the Salzburg train about Captain
Theodor Koch of the Hapag Line. Koch was one of those
gentleman-captains whose excellent appearance and perfect
manners assured them of a distinguished career, and to whom
were entrusted the big ships on the North Atlantic route to New
York. I imagine that many Englishmen will remember this elegant
and well-poised officer. Koch, then, who had been commander of
a corvette in the Imperial Navy, was in this war put in charge of
one of the British islands in the Channel which we had occupied.
But late last autumn, a high-ranking Gestapo functionary appeared
on the island. A long palaver followed, voices were raised, and at
the end Koch took his service revolver and shot himself.

The strange part of the story is that orderlies in the ante-room outside, who were able to hear fragments of the conversation, distinctly heard repeated mention of a tunnel. My Hamburg travelling companion, about whom I would very much like to have more information, evidently could have told me more if he had wanted to, but refused.

For my part, I will believe that the circle has been squared before I will believe in this tunnel. But what *is* reality is the fear these Nazi desperadoes have of the fate awaiting them. They will try anything, including going to the moon, to escape it.

So much for the rather sparse sum of my lonely days this winter. What else? Recently, whom should I be seated next to at the Regina Hotel but former Reichsbank president Herr Hjalmar Schacht himself, now fallen into disgrace, a veritable cobra swollen with poison, delivering himself rather loudly – loudly enough so I could hear, anyway – of the opinion that if inflation were avoided now, he would gladly begin to believe in perpetual motion. The next day I joined a table of regular customers at the Café Helbig, at which the argument of the Catholic theologians present centred about various techniques of punishment. For the Herr Propaganda Minister, an appearance, naked, in the monkey cage at the Hellabrunn Zoo at increased prices was proposed, but with popular prices on special days. For the Great Man himself, nothing less than a world tour, in a cage 'with rings on his fingers and bells on his toes'. The precedent here would be the punishment of Bockelson, king of the Anabaptists, whom the medieval authorities had put in a cage and then exchanged among one another like a canary, so that each in turn could have him on hand during coffee to enliven things with his gallows humour and saucy *bons mots* before being put to death.

I was rather entertained by all this. The prospect of seeing Hitler singing the 'Horst Wessel Lied', naked on the Broadway stage – this idea, aside from providing a certain personal satisfaction, has deep, and it appears to me, politically practical significance. There should be room in the coming German revolution for laughter after almost a decade in which this has been forbidden, as a safety valve through which some of the pent-up rage can be vented. Close this valve, as was done in 1919, with 'Law and Order' and the explosive charge will blow into the face of the maker of political fireworks. This martyrdom that is Hitlerism might have been spared us if at that time and even if for the most conservative reasons, we had faced up to a thorough-going revolution, and had allowed the masses to rid themselves of their anger, and roar until they had tired themselves out.

I have had a long discussion with M., who for years has been prevented by the Nazis from teaching the social sciences, about the physiology and pathology of mass-man. I can clearly remember having talked about the same thing – the fact that in the last 140 years the population of Europe has increased two and a half times – with Spengler a number of times. Of course, Spengler, with his one-track mind, put everything down to the legalising of children born out of wedlock and the marriages of second and third sons of peasants who had previously become soldiers or priests. But I, then as now, was forced to come to different, more frightening conclusions.

M.'s thinking on the subject turns to the cheek-by-jowl life of modern-day man which technology has brought with it. I cannot rest content with this, because mass-man is not at all to be found exclusively among the working class. In fact, he is perhaps less common among the workers than among certain sections of the bourgeoisie who do not at all live in crowded conditions. In addition, I observed that in the two precedents for the contemporary situation known to us – Imperial Rome and the Inca state prior to the landing of Columbus – this sudden, violent transformation into a mass-man horde was not at all indicative of robust health. It was symptomatic of decline and fall, connected, in the period of decline at the time of Caracalla, with worship of the magical placenta, with tangible social decay and threatening physical destruction.

This is mass-man: arrogantly striding onto the stage of history, yet already sick; suddenly the centre of all attention, but incapable of maintaining himself for long; destined to disappear in the kind of ghostly emptying of the stage described around AD 400 by a Greek journalist in Rome – the city once crowded with millions of inhabitants had become a little country town of a few thousand people. Its Forum was now a cornfield, out of which the hermae rose here and there among the sheaves of corn.

Is there anyone left these days who really believes that this proliferation of people is merely a modern fulfilment of the ancient injunction to 'be fruitful and multiply'? There is a vast gulf between that injunction and its contemporary fulfilment; the crowded conditions of our large cities do not account for the increase in population we are now seeing. No, this population explosion has more the look of a worldwide plague. Even my peaceful village here, as I learn from church records, has quadrupled in population over the last hundred years. The result of the discoveries of science? I am more inclined to believe that present-day science, in its scope and power, in its tendency to replace the precious natural product by a synthetic, a chemical poison, is a *product* of mass-man, and not the other way around. I believe that the drive of present-day science to replace the tried and true products of yesterday by the cheap and standardised article, in radios, in Volkswagens, in rayon stockings, is further proof of this cause and effect.

And what about today's so-called 'better health standards' – the elimination of contagious disease, and the raising of life expectancy; the disappearance of wasp-waists and whalebone-bellies, and the emergence of the 'New German Look'? Oh, I wish we had them all back, those bad old times! At least, for God's sake, now and then, you could find a human face, something of the old, unprettified German among those admittedly inferior types. If only by some lucky stroke of history we could just get rid of this visage of hysterical emptiness which is the typical physiognomy of Hitlerism!

And to come back to the matter of increased life expectancy: this is largely due to the incubation of basically unfit children, and the elimination of the examination of the newborn that was once customary to determine if the infant was sound in mind and body. I have already mentioned the high incidence of sexual malfunction of male and female athletes noted by the doctors who treated them. This is nature's own way of warning that it does not want the continuation of human types one-sidedly developed in terms of the somatic.

At the same time these hollow men are produced in ever greater quantities, there is a stunting of the feeling for the metaphysical, a feeling nature placed in man at the beginning of time. There is no caste, either of priests or of kings any longer, nor does the law-giver and judge any longer carry the priestly authority. There is no metaphysical focal point today, around which all the varieties of human experience can crystallise. The result is that no speculative philosophy worthy of the name exists, nor could it: The sages at the universities presently engaged in this discipline are akin to a group of highly respected night-watchmen who are limited to playing an endless old-man's game of taroc with the same tired, used-up formulas.

The treasure house of form that is art has been broken into, and its contents have been defiled by much fingering. The flight of German architects into the New Realism has ended in an architecture that is more unrealistic than the full-beard of yesteryear. The attempt to build a church becomes a blasphemy in stone, and the composer of a string quartet ends with something so pretentious and so boring despite all its agitatedness that it becomes mere noise at the sounding of a Mozart passage.

Despite the fact that even coral strives for form, that nature abhors the amorphous as the original indecency, mankind goes steadily on sinking deeper and deeper into formlessness, hatred of all form. The ideal is now that thoroughly bovine condition in which any distinction given to rank or profession is considered ridiculous, and all is confusion: the professor looks like a sportsman, the waiter like an aristocrat, the aristocrat like a head-waiter. The businessman raises thoroughbreds, and the cavalry officer speculates in Rand mining stock. It has come to the point where streetwalkers and perhaps burglars are the only remaining groups who still have about them something like a professional distinctiveness.

And what a sweaty fingering and pawing of things which were formerly spoken of only in awe and wonder, how they profane the titles and trappings of honour formerly accorded only to the immortals, the heroes, the great thinkers! In Germany now, you need only be a veteran of a beer-hall brawl, to get the same title of field marshal that was given Moltke for the victory at Sedan. If you combine the face of a horse trader with Nazi Party membership, you are eligible to be hailed as a 'statesman'. Goethe would have burned his writings if he had imagined a time would come when people like Herybert Menzel and Joseph Magnus Wehner would be celebrated as writers; Frederick the Great would not merely have sought death at Kunersdorf, but would certainly have found it, if he had been able to foresee that the day would come when he would be placed side by side on a wooden plaque with the man from the furnished room on Barerstrasse – shameful juxtaposition, a disgrace to Germany! In their time of greatness, the Germans produced the unforgettable images of the Mother of God and the knightly dragon-killer. Now, we are blessed with Hitler Youth versions of St George, of BDM versions of the Madonna, who resemble the ideal about as much as Goebbels resembles Dorian Gray and Otto Gebühr is like Frederick the Great.

I am, despite the impression I may have conveyed, not in the least contending that this dirtying and weakening of all higher concepts is connected solely with the Nazis or the German termite heap. I see this sea of mass-men lapping at the last islands of our culture in practically every country, and I see that, England perhaps excepted, the besieged are ready to surrender. As though this defeat was something ordained by fate, when really, by recognition of the reality and by acceptance of martyrdom, it can be avoided! This is no longer a matter of inevitable evolution, as it was in 1789. What we have here is a bid for power by the degenerates, and it can be fought with the weapons of one's own ability to endure and to hold fast to belief in the truth. If necessary, even martyrdom can serve in this battle.

I will never change my belief that mass-man is by no means identical with the proletariat. The mass type is now to be found much oftener in the boardrooms of the large corporations and among the sons and daughters of rich industrialists than among workers. The fact is that we are dealing here with pestilence, some unnameable kind of biological dissolution, that began in the higher reaches of our social structure.

I believe that my call to resistance and a naysaying to mass-man are justified in the face of this diagnosis and this prognosis, based on mass-man's biological instability and the fact that his periods of existence on the earth have always been short. I have already talked about the mysterious connection that I have found to exist between the expansion of population and the increased emphasis on the somatic, between the modern termite heap and its increasing proneness to virulent tumours like some grim, God-inflicted plague. Cancer cell and mass-man: the same defective biological structure, the same tendency towards early death and decay, the same reproductive explosiveness, and the same anarchic emergence of previously fixed forms. This disease is sweeping down over us today with the tidal speed of the Black Plague. Surely, this fact alone reveals its deep-seated connection with the thing which is now threatening man's entire culture?

I am optimistic enough to believe that this black cloud which came up over our heads during the last century will some day disappear, even if only after years of apocalyptic horror. Economically, mass-man is an impossibility, as will be proved as soon as industry can blanket the world with its products. Then, this ridiculous overpopulation will be shown for what it is – excessive, and therefore untenable, as untenable and purposeless as feudalism was when it had fulfilled its historic function at the end of the eighteenth century. Mass-man is a non-viable organism threatened by all the non-rational developments now gathering momentum, like storm clouds on our horizon. It is entirely conceivable that before this happens, before the storm now in preparation actually comes, that Spengler's grim vision, in which he saw the last violin lying broken on the ground, the last copy of Mozart quartets going up in flames, may be fulfilled. But what is quite impossible is that a creature derived from rationality and so overdeveloped under its sway will survive a new invasion of the non-rational or the anti-rational. And the endless spiritual vacuity of our time makes this invasion well-nigh automatic.

Life does not allow mindlessness, it punishes a disturbance of the necessary harmony between body-functioning and mind-functioning by death – and death remains a constant, no matter what else is changed inside this bordello mass-man has constructed. This war based on the revolt of the masses may destroy the Gothic cathedrals and silence forever Bach's 'Chaconne': but a horde of degenerate football players will not survive the fire they started.

February 1942

Nationalistic history-writing: In Germany, the lies have a blonde character. Nationalism: a state of mind in which you do not love your own country as much as you hate somebody *else's*.

And now mass-man has forged for himself the perfect tool to provide explanations of the most difficult problems – a solution that is plausible, will never change, and can be immediately understood by everybody. A recent issue of the *Schwarze Korps*[56] magazine informs us that there is in the lives of men no such entity as 'tragedy', not for the SS anyway, and furthermore – the following is a quotation – 'Tragedy is a condition *first discovered by the Pope* for the subjection of mankind.'

But that is the provoking thing about these people: they foist this barbarism on us, and then try to make us content with it by having us adopt their own mass-man inability to distinguish between things. We are to end by no longer knowing that the whole of their 'technical comfort' amounts to nothing more than one gigantic swindle, a shabby little ersatz-life, and that the mass-produced amenities they are providing us with are about as much like the genuine article as aniline colours are like a rainbow.

Or do they really think they are going to stop us from making distinctions and reduce everything to dead level – equate a Brueghelian feast of the past with a modern meal out of cans; the rewards of an auto trip with that of a walking tour; the costly silk stockings of yesterday, and the rayon stockings of today's office girls – all calculated to turn the beholder into a misogynist.

Are we supposed to believe that Japanese woodcuts before and since the development of aniline colours are the same? Or that grandfather's trip through Italy, planned to take two years and last him a lifetime, is to be equated with the four-week, express train 'covering' of Italy from Verona to Taranto, during which mass-man 'sees' it all, and then has to go to a sanatorium to recover? Is the sexual awakening which used to come *brevi manu* in the haystack to be paralleled by a lecture course given by the Reich's Führer of Women, Scholtz-Klinck – with or without practical demonstrations?

Earlier, when I talked about professional or class distinctions, I spoke of that honourable profession, the streetwalkers, as being the last to retain distinctive identifying characteristics. Now, I must hasten to retract even this bit of encouragement. It now appears that even sin must be sacrificed on the altar of progress. The latest word is that National Socialist Germany is about to establish a Reich's Council of Prostitutes, complete with parliamentary debate, trial by a jury of one's peers, and scientifically prepared career courses. This would be under the protection of the highest authority, a responsibility most conveniently assumed by the Reich's Propaganda Minister.

As a matter of fact, there is nothing lacking here for the formation of a modern German labour union – with one minor exception, perhaps: only you are missing, Mr Industrialist. Only you.

11 March 1942

From a reading of Schopenhauer: In order that I may better understand the intellectual quality of the Germans, and thus be better prepared for events to come, I have made note of several points to keep in mind in future.

1. Fichte is still, forty years after his first book, being placed on a level with his master, Kant – as though they had something in common.
2. Lichtenberg's works not only did not go through a second edition – they are now, thirty-two years after their appearance, practically being given away, while the writings of Messrs Krug, Hegel, etc., have gone through a number of editions.

For some reason the thought comes into my mind that when patriotism enters the realm of science it should be taken by the collar like a dirty little boy and thrown out.

There is a contention now being made that the Germans invented gunpowder. I, however, find this difficult to believe.

Thoughts after reading Heine on Germany (*From Kant to Hegel*): Christianity tempered somewhat the brutality of the Germanic delight in war, but was completely unable basically to change the feeling, and if the day comes when that moderating symbol, the Cross, loses its power, the senseless, berserk rage of which the Nordic poets write and sing so much will break loose again. Then, the old stone gods will rise up out of the ruins and rub the dust of a thousand years out of their eyes. And then Thor will spring forth, raising his mighty hammer, and smash into nothingness the Gothic cathedrals....

I warn you against Kantians, Fichteans, and Natural Philosophers – do not laugh. I expect the same revolution to occur in the world of material reality as has already taken place in the world of the spirit. The conception is father to the act, and precedes it as lightning precedes the thunder. Of course, this is *German* thunder, and therefore rather ponderous and slow-moving. But it will come. And when you hear the boom of it – such a sound as has never been heard before in the history of the world, then you will know: it has come, finally. And then, there will be a roar as will bring eagles plummeting out of the sky, and send lions in the most distant parts of Africa hurrying for their royal holes, tails between their legs. The things that will happen then in Germany will make the French Revolution look like a harmless idyll by comparison.

May 1942

Everybody is wailing about the destruction of Lübeck and Rostock, and nobody could possibly be more unhappy about the loss of these Gothic masterpieces than I am.

But what happened here? Thirty years ago, Rostock was still the peaceful, self-contained market town of a prosperous farming area. Then, the idea was conceived of filling both Rostock and Lübeck with armament factories. These plants could just as well have been located in some uninteresting and architecturally worthless little towns. But the engineers did not want to be bored in provincial towns, and the burgomasters wanted to bring 'progress' to their communities. The result was the same as happened in Munich, which can thank Herr Krupp for the fact that it was blessed with its first great industrial complex during World War I, and that this was followed by others.

So now people are crying over two cathedrals which we will never have again, and which were wrecked by the industrial monomania which is the source of all our unhappiness. They weep, but they do not beat their own breasts. What about the household tools, the screwdrivers and handsaws that are kept in costly baroque cabinets – and the irreplaceable crystal glassware used to impress one's hunting guests? After the war, will these engineers, these War Production Board generals, these burgomasters and community leaders be called to account for the unspeakable frivolity with which they gambled away the treasures entrusted to them?

It does not appear so. For years now, these pestilential north

German corporations have been eating away at the quiet valley where I live, driving out the farmers, planting in their place social instability, poverty, discontent. And then these people have the truly monumental gall to claim credit for having brought 'progress' to the region, just like the Lübeck and Rostock burgo-masters!

Building has been going on for years here on a huge underground depot for munitions and poison gas, farmers have been expropriated without payment, and a vast stock of chemical filth of unthinkably terrible power is being buried here, endangering an entire region of what was peaceful countryside. Every night, I hear the shunting about of immense trains carrying gas bombs and similar weapons – a single air attack could turn the whole beautiful region into a hell of fire and gas.

The following is typical of what is happening. The technician in charge of this poison stockpile, a gentleman from Prussia who left the honourable profession of fireman to begin his rise to the rank of captain, one night began drunkenly shooting at the guards at the depot, and when they protested, hit them with his fists. The next morning he attempted to bribe the corporals who had been on guard. The enlisted men, however, all Bavarians, simply laughed at him. He was reported, and disappeared overnight, swallowed up somewhere in the cogs and wheels of the Nazi military machine. Since, except for this mishap, he was perfect in every way, he will probably reappear somewhere else: this time, perhaps, as satrap of a little supply point in Poland, where he will be master of life and death over the inhabitants, and can shoot undisturbed at living targets.

So much for the functionaries who are named to administer chemical hells, and who through some slight error can cause the most beastly of deaths to an entire region – man and animal, tree and grass.

As regards the bombing of Rostock, a relative of mine who is a well-known gynaecologist lost his private clinic on the first night of the attack. The second night, his apartment was destroyed, along with all his possessions. Pyjama-clad, the sixty-year-old man managed to squeeze through a window in his cellar and escape – his bare existence was all he could salvage out of a lifetime of hard work.

I have word that Ernst Niekisch,[57] who was sentenced to life imprisonment by the Nazis four years ago after a sensation-filled trial closely followed abroad, has been murdered in prison. Niekisch, a simple schoolmaster of Bavarian origin, was, nevertheless, one of the cleverest and most unusual men I have ever met. The winter of 1919, during the Munich Revolt, I was a voluntary prisoner in the Bayrischer Hof Hotel, together with fifty other gentlemen, all adherents like me of old Prince Leopold of Bavaria. Niekisch, a prominent political figure and chairman of the Soldiers' Council, did everything he could to ensure decent, I might almost say *gentlemanly*, treatment for his prisoners. Niekisch had an obvious partiality for everything that connoted *ancien régime* – as contrasted with capitalist – and the result was that we ended by having our own roulette wheel, even, on which we gambled away the last of our reserve money, ringing old silver thalers from before 1870.

The second time I saw him, in 1930, Niekisch had become the leader of a small, but fanatically devoted group on the order of the Tannenberg Bund of Ludendorff. This assortment of ex-Army officers, Free Corps adherents, and starving students was supported by an extraordinarily well edited newspaper, the organ of the Russophile section of the General Staff. Of course, this involved them in deadly conflict with the Hitlerites, who were apoplectic in their hatred of the Russians.

I was twice a guest at Niekisch's 'Days', held behind barred doors at the old Leuchtenberg Castle, or else under tent cover in the midst of the Thuringian forest. The programme included frugal, Army-style meals, sports in the morning, and very clever talks in the evening, given for the most heterogeneous company I have ever seen. Included were secret agents for all parties, right to left; poverty-stricken little high-school and college students who, after long and weary peregrinations across the Reich had finally pitched their tents here; dubious left-overs from the Rossbach[58] group; stigmatised former divisional chaplains; superannuated generals; undercover Reichswehr officers; political scum; and even a few SA men of the opposition wing which was destroyed two years afterwards in the Röhm affair.

Niekisch himself, round as a ball, with the piercing look of a Hippocrates and eyes which looked narrowly and somewhat pessimistically out into the world, was, of course, anything but an 'arch-traitor'. But he was doomed from the time he began striking with biting irony and ferocious hatred at the Nazis and at Hitler himself. And his fate was sealed by the lack of character of the men on the General Staff. Since 1918, utilitarianism, political opportunism, and the breaking of one's word have become something like the tradition among the new breed on the General Staff. It was taken for granted that Niekisch's backers would drop him the moment Hitler set himself up as the Germany's Man of Destiny and one-man military government.

The whole of Niekisch's high treason undoubtedly was because of the fact that his publication, which for some reason was allowed to go on until 1935, aroused the displeasure of the Nazis' evil genius, Herr Rosenberg, and that Niekisch took every opportunity to poke fun at the Great Manitou – who has now taken to comparing himself to Scipio Africanus, and even to Cromwell.

Irony in regard to the dictator can bring death to the man who cannot help expressing it. But I wonder: Do the judges of Niekisch who four years ago took on themselves the responsibility for his imprisonment and therefore of his political murder – do they feel quite secure inside their skins?

June 1942

In Stuttgart to see my publisher, I met an old lady who survived the sinking of the *Titanic* thirty years ago, a catastrophe shrouded in obscurity to this day. This lady told me about an incredible thing that happened while the boat was sinking, and as the water was already lapping at the promenade deck and the boats were being let down into the water. At this very moment, the ship's stewards were going about the deck carrying trays full of sandwiches, and murmuring, 'May I offer you a sandwich?' – never-failingly good-humoured, remaining on duty to the end. Here, in a place where one would hardly look for it, a representation of the soul of an Englishman and with it an episode worthy of Joseph Conrad.

I have been with my dying Clemens von Franckenstein, whose cancer is in its terminal stage. I went with him for a consultation with my doctor, since Clemens imagined it might do some good: this proud man, who only a short time ago delighted in his own physical power, and exuded strength, and who today could not get into the car without my help; he sat in a waiting room filled to suffocation with fat bourgeois and hysterical actresses and the piti-less light of a burning hot day.

Naturally, this consultation could have only fictive value; natu-rally, he knew that his condition was hopeless; naturally, it was all a little comedy he was playing, conceived out of tenderness and consideration for his wife, in an attempt somehow to allay her desolation a little.

There we sat, playing out to the end our macabre roles, and

then had breakfast with Walterspiel, who did not recognise Clé, so much had he changed. We knew that we had come to the end of a friendship of thirty years, that we were sitting opposite each other for the last time.

Never again to enjoy those analyses of yours, never again to be amazed by the contrast: at first sight, the impression of cool poise – and then the gentle heart that lay behind, most ready to help.

We went to see Clé's cousin, Erwein Schönborn, who is a patient at the Neuwittelsbach Clinic. His letters seemed to indicate that he was not seriously ill. Instead, I found to my horror that he is terribly changed – shrunk to a skeleton, marked with death as Clé is.

Now with Clé, formerly a partner in conversation that was generally ironic, that tended even to cynicism, the conversation took on a tone I had never heard before. There was a note of gentleness in the talk of the two men, a kind of brotherly consideration, a delicate and melancholy opening of the heart peculiar to those bound by blood who now are separating for life.

I am going to lose both of them. They were my companions and my friends, they represented for me the ideal of the kind of man almost extinct in Germany. Far-seeing men, men of the world; large-hearted, great-spirited friends of all that is human; my fellow workers, I hoped, in the task of building a new Germany, new from the ground up.

Outside, the pitilessly full life of summer, and the harsh sounds of the city we loved so much, which now has become so strange. Inside, the dying men, and the gentle voice of suffering and of hopelessness; sad and heavy recollection of the past, past skiing adventures, past discussions, past festivities, all our shared experiences.

I went home, deeply alone, unutterably impoverished. It is as though all the light has gone out of the world. It is as though our lives are an ebbing tide that recedes farther and farther down a sandbank – and you think that the tide will never come back again, never in your life. It is as though the sun has become smaller, as though, one by one, the stars are going out.

There are those blessed ones who understand the mystery of God's dealing with his children: Joseph Conrad, in *The End of the Tether*, in the story of the martyrdom of Whaley, the blinded sea captain – Joseph Conrad, whose work, I need scarcely add, has been placed on the Index by Herr Joseph Goebbels....

But I, on this summer night, hot as cobalt, have lost myself. The distant worlds are enclosed in icy separation. The Throne of God is even farther away, and with it the great Book of Wisdom, whose pages my friends will soon be reading. My life is loneliness, and the growing awareness that it must be so – loneliness among a people whom Satan has overcome, and the awareness that only by suffering can the future be changed.

Isolation, with one last chance given one in this life: the chance to affirm truth by one's death.

But you, who are still living in the world of yesterday, that comfortable world, that world where sound still exists: do you know anything, really, about this blackness in which we live? Do you know that the way to the Absolute is through the deep vale of suffering? And do you know that only out of our passion and out of our suffering can the seed be sown for the new day?

30 October 1942

I watched the first bombing of Munich from a hotel room in Alt-Ötting, where I have come to examine the material on Tilly located here; a hideous red glare, transforming the autumn night and its full moon. I heard in the distance the muffled booms, and it was calculated that since the bombs were dropping eighty kilometres away, it had taken three minutes for the sound to carry – three minutes during which the victims at the scene had been gasping and gagging and dying. Finally, the whole of the sky to the west was a gigantic sheet of fire.

In the days that followed, people spoke of fantastic losses, largely due to suffocation. People were still being dug out five days later, wedged in among fallen beams and rubble, where they had been unable to move. And then there were the dead, whose faces still bore the marks of their last agonies.

Since many high-ranking Nazis have private and luxuriously appointed residences in Solln, which the English evidently know, that unlucky suburb was bombed three times in succession. Werner Bergengruen, who lives there, lost all his manuscripts, his collections, the whole of his possessions when his house went. He was seen the next day in a state of shock and despair, perched on the pile of ruins that had been his house, offering passers-by the few things that had survived the holocaust: a Latin primer, a small bronze, a couple of Chinese *objets d'art*. Alongside was a hand-lettered placard announcing that this was a special sale by a German writer of the remains of his possessions. The police tried to drive him off, but he defended himself so energetically, and the crowd standing about was so sympathetic, that the gendarmes had to retreat.

Herr Hitler happened to be in Munich the night of the air-raid, and before the alarm had been sounded for the *misera plebs*, he was already safely tucked away in a private shelter complete with rugs on the floors, baths and, reportedly, even a movie projection-room. Thus, while hundreds and hundreds of people buried under rubble struggled horribly to breathe, he might well have been watching a movie....

Naturally, he announced after it was over that everything would be rebuilt, far better than before. Presumably, after some young Canadian turns the Frauenkirche into a pile of rubble, he will assign Herr Speer to help us reconcile ourselves to the loss of this and other cathedrals. I would assume that he is secretly delighted over the loss of our Gothic masterpieces, since he has always wanted to become one of the immortals of architecture – hasn't he already threatened to pull down the Theatinerkirche, the Hofgarten arcades, and the Leuchtenberg Palace to make room for a colossal opera? Here, at Chiem, we are supposed to be getting a Leaders' School, a kind of stud farm for future chancellors, which would run for a kilometre and a half along the eastern shore of this peaceful lake. The whole quiet shoreline would be transformed into a mass of stone, dominated by a tower 130 metres high. One assumes that the task of his personal architects is to carry out orders, and keep quiet.

With the malignant narrow-mindedness of the man marked by the Devil, he hates everything that has grown up straight and healthy, and the opposite of himself. With the hatred of the illegitimate, he hates everything that belongs among the precious elements of our tradition, and which does not flatter his vanity. Is it really too much to say, when we view this dangerous gorilla, that we are prisoners of a Neanderthal man who has got loose from his chain?

And so we continue to vegetate in our life of shame, our life of dishonour, our life of lies. And our protest, at least the protest of our cowardly bourgeoisie, is in the retelling of old jokes about the regime, while their remaining days are spent swallowing propaganda.

Following a series of articles placed by Goebbels in the newspapers, the wife of a tenant came to see me in fear and trembling. In Jesus' name, how was she to protect her children? They were all going to be dragged off to be raised in English, American, or Russian orphan asylums, according to newspapers! *Nota bene*, this woman spent several years in America, as a laundress; she still speaks a little English, and she has a number of quite warm recollections of Boston – yet she believes these stories about the foreign devils. Really, this people, only yesterday so intelligent and discriminating, seems to have been overcome by a disease of the mind. They now believe everything they are told, provided it is done with sufficient aplomb.

The latest is a story concocted by Goebbels that our so-called 'Leader' appeared in some town without previously announcing that he was coming. Nevertheless, there the whole town was, lined up awaiting him, as though some kind of radiance emanating from him had made itself felt in advance! If an official of Imperial or Weimar Germany had dared put out such a story, the shout of laughter that would have gone up would have sufficed to send him flying out of office, and would have followed him for the rest of his days. But this is broadcast by the networks, and believed, and digested, without a soul's daring to so much as smile.

Literally everything is believed today, if it is printed, or broadcast, or publicly proclaimed under official auspices. If Herr Göring suddenly, and with the requisite blare of trumpets, proclaimed one of his hunting dogs King of Bavaria, I really believe that the same people who only yesterday were so proud of their differentness *vis-à-vis* the north German ant heap, and so jealously guardian of their own special characteristics, would shout hurrah and bow down.

There is some eerie, impending thing in the air, the whole physical structure of our lives seems to have broken down under the weight of these never-ending lies. For the last nine years, since the coming of Hitlerism, the summers have been concepts on a calendar only, and have drowned us in rainfall like the original Flood. Year after year, the vintages have failed. The botanists say that certain plants which normally bloom in the autumn now come up in spring, while there are spring-blooming plants which now emerge in late autumn. I have heard from zoologists on the Eastern Front, in the northern Caucasus, that tropical snakes formerly native to India are now to be found in the vicinity of the Volga, on the threshold of Europe. Thus, everything is out of joint, the usual order of things has been overturned. And what is this plague that now afflicts Germany, but a disgusting symptom of the same thing?

Clé died in August, bitterly, painfully, calling in his death agony to the brother in England he loved most dearly. Eight weeks before that, while black storm clouds lay over the little house on the Pilsensee, he had played for me my favourite song from his opera, *Li Tai-Pe*, the melancholy Song of the Cormorant. I sat beside him, heartsick at those fingers grown thin as matchsticks. Then, in the midst of his playing, blue flame shot between us as lightning ran down a conductor. The lights went out, the fuses were shattered into pieces. It was as though nature was already separating us.

Now, I expect every day to hear of the death of his cousin, Erwein von Schönborn, who is in agony in Munich.

Yesterday, I was discussing with H. the changing forms of man's cruelty, with particular reference to the horror the Eastern Front has now become, and I remembered something which happened to me almost forty years ago, but which is still, today, fearfully present to me in all its grisly details. I was still a cadet at the time, on a short leave in Königsberg, and a friend of mine from school days invited me to go with him to a session on anatomy.

Most of the students were away for the holidays, and only one of the greasy-looking dissecting tables was in use. This was being serviced by an old attendant with a bushy, dirty, gray beard, who was busying himself, at the moment I walked in, with removing the head from a newly arrived corpse. This head had been completely smashed by a revolver shot.

I fled, but this old man followed me like a vampire, brandishing his fatty knife, and there, in the corridor, related the story of the corpse. The case was that of a homosexual druggist, who had shot his lover and would-be blackmailer, and then had killed himself. As no one claimed the despised remains, the one-time druggist had ended in the dissecting-room.

Some cynical twist of fate brought me into contact with the same corpse two years later. Now a medical student, I entered the same room for my first session in dissection, and found before me the livid flesh of the former apothecary. I recognised it at once as the remains of the man who had been brought by his equivocal inclinations to this miserable and apocryphal end. If there had been any doubt, the attendant removed it. That hideous old man served as a kind of ambulatory obituary notice for the poor, disgraced figures on the tables.

I will never forget the feeling I had when my hand touched the lumpy flesh for the first time, nor the first cut I made into this flesh. I looked around me. With me, around the same corpse, were three other young students. They faced the same problem as I, and their honest little-boy faces reflected the same attempt to fight down their horror and disgust. The whole room was filled with such boys, standing about their hideously bedecked tables, former students of Plato and the verses of the *Iliad* who had deserted the disciplines of humanism and now found themselves faced with the necessity to jump down into the foul air of decomposition where analysis takes place....

We would negotiate this leap successfully, and the proof that we would was reflected in the ironic expressions of the instructors and their assistants, and the still more ironical faces of the graduate students. I can remember only one of the beginners present who threw his knife away and never came back. Each of the rest of us set himself and began to work, began at the cost of a shameful metamorphosis of himself, and a subjection of himself to this metamorphosis, which I recall today as a shameful and troubling memory. I do not doubt that all of those present were the well-brought-up sons of a middle-class whose position was still unchallenged; I still correspond with several of them, and I know that in their leisure hours they read Baudelaire and find relaxation in an occasional string quartet. I know also that their feeling of horror when they view the orgy of brutality which is today filling the world is akin to mine.

But what could we do but drown our disgust in cynicism? Immediately, from the time of that first incision, the entire room was filled with obscene joking, with the whistling of popular tunes, and with laughter that was intended to be casual, but that had a worried and cramped sound. This went on for weeks, and even today, almost a half century later, the memory fills me with shame. The jokes we made as we went about our macabre business became daily more obscene, and more and more grisly comedy was forced out of the positions taken by the corpses – poor puppets that they were – and the obscene postures that would have been implied if there had been life in them. That was the only period of my life when existence here on earth presented itself to me as a mean little game played by forces whose nature was raw and massive as a steamroller; a dreary comedy whose title was *Inter faeces et urinas*, and the depressing conclusion, in the style of the tragedy of Wozzeck.

Of course, there came a time when I gained new understanding, and realised that all this had really been nothing but our defence against the horrible. But what defence is possible now, against the things now rising from the grave, the ghostly train now passing across the dark heavens of these late autumn days?

For, from Paris comes word that the Père Lachaise cemetery has been dug up in a search for Heine's bones, and since no bones were found, and something had to be done, the mold in the grave was excavated and strewn to the four winds. And an informant who was at the scene at the time has told me about the murder of Herr von Kahr, who was trampled to death by SS beasts in the courtyard of the Marienbad Hotel, in Munich: twenty-year-old louts and a seventy-year-old man.

And H., with whom I philosophised today about man's inhumanity to man? He has just come back from the Eastern Front, and witnessed the massacre at K., where 30,000 Jews were slaughtered.

This was done in a single day, in the space of an hour, perhaps, and when machine-gun bullets gave out, flamethrowers were used. And spectators hurried to the event from all over the city, off-duty troops, young fellows with the milk-complexion of the young – the children of men, who also, nineteen or twenty years ago, were lying in cribs and gaily bubbling and reaching for the brightly coloured ring hanging just above! Oh, degradation, oh, life without honour, oh, thin shell that separates us from the lost souls in whom Satan burns!

You judge us and find us wanting, and we, here, suffer in loneliness and dread. You point at us, and at our lack of resistance, and we know that the resistants have died unknown in filthy bunkers, and that the blood of martyrs has been spilled to no purpose, that deeds to match Charlotte Corday's have been done, and never heard of. The Devil is loose, and it is God Himself who has unloosed him. 'And the Lord will give him great power.' And we can only guess at why He has done this, or why He has chosen this land as His stage, or what lies in store for us, behind His curtain.

But still the night lies black over our heads, and we suffer, we suffer as you never shall suffer, no, not on your deathbed.

Beware, the man who would make light of our suffering!

February 1943

The news of the Anglo-American landing in Africa spread with a speed that amazed me. Despite the ban on listening to the Allied radio, the news spread within an hour. And I was even more amazed, that gray November day, to see the reaction the news produced. Everyone seemed glad about this decisive change in the course of the war, which meant the defeat of his own country, and Bavarians had the added consideration to ponder that the fighting must eventually reach the Alps.

And yet the whole town – the whole region, really – was as exhilarated as though everybody had drunk a bottle of champagne. Suddenly, people walked straighter, and their faces shone, and it was as though a long, hard winter had been endured and now the first warm wind was blowing over the ice. Everyone sensed that a ghostly hand had nailed the death warrant of the Nazis to the wall, and this had as salutary an effect on the bad as it did on the good. The local schoolteacher, like all his profession an eager preacher of the Nazi Word, suddenly and demonstratively began using the old greeting *'Grüss Gott'* instead of *'Heil Hitler'*. The district's chief Nazi called a meeting to plead that people for God's sake stop threatening to burn down his house, since he had, after all, only been carrying out orders from the Party.

That was the effect of the news on our villages. Hitler blustered, but behind the rhetoric was the shriek of fear. The days are past when people viewed him as a Saviour and were not ashamed; past, when, as actually happened in Prussian Protestant churches, his portrait, that perfect likeness of Dorian Gray, stood on the altar next to his book, that Machiavelli for chambermaids. The nimbus of the god is gone. Slowly, the canaille is beginning to come forward with the bill for the vast deception which has been foisted on it.

There is a kind of nasty satisfaction on everyone's face these days, the look of pious virtue has vanished overnight. The Nazi emblem has disappeared from coat lapels, and in government offices it is now common practice for officials who years ago were punished for hostility towards the Party to have the fact put on official record. Near here, an arbitration board ordered a farmer whose land had been partially expropriated for the 'war effort' – without compensation, naturally – to testify before it. The man, seized by an onrush of fury, called the arbitrators a pack of scoundrels, the regime a band of thieves, and the Highest of all, a 'crazy pain-in-the-ass'. Then he left, banging the door behind him. The authorities were so perplexed by this strong language, coming after years of silence, that the man is still free.

Meanwhile, things are getting better from one day to the next. There is a shortage of chloroform and morphine in the Army hospitals. Doctors are protesting the fact that hospital trains are arriving in which the wounded lie on stinking straw in ice-cold freight cars. In Berlin, an entire unit of diabetics has perished for lack of insulin.

I have been reading the memoirs of the German Crown Prince, about the period 1870-1, and once again I find the circumstances connected with the founding of the Reich wholly shattering.

There are the casual conversations, marked by the most disdainful kind of language, which determined what the symbol of the Reich was to be – as though this were a trade-mark for a product to prevent falling hair. There is Bismarck's statement regarding the colours, that as far as he was concerned, the new colours of the Reich could be 'green and gold, like a dance-hall's, with "dancing tonight" printed above'.

Is this really the way a Reich is founded? Does the rebirth of a nation happen this way? This is how a new coffee export firm is founded, this is the debate of future partners on the by-laws of a new stock company – this is how you nail together an economically feasible unit which will then try to earn the name of Reich!

And everywhere in the Crown Prince's journals, the lack of consideration, the arrogance of its royal author – a foretaste of what is to come with the son, Wilhelm II. Between the lines, one senses the disappearance of solidity in German life, the growing rapacity of the robber-barons, the cynical denial of a great spiritual heritage. There is nothing here of that mysterious seed which lies at the heart of every healthy state, that deeply hidden chamber where every healthily developed nation has enshrined the things which are 'not of this world'.

No, this Reich was compounded of a dash of duelling-club romanticism and the gymnastics originated by that 'Father of Gymnastics', Ludwig Jahn, a touch of Hegel and a healthy slice of Friedrich List – all this in a rich broth of greed, greed of an entire generation, for riches to be had as fast and as painlessly as possible. Wasn't it basically sound instinct which led Ludwig of Bavaria to refuse the title of Kaiser, and were those men of my grandfather's generation who shrugged and turned away from the new firm nothing but reactionary cranks? This Prussian Reich derived from the will-to-power and arrogance of a colony which had seized control of the mother country, and the thing could have come to no good end for this reason alone.

This Reich was dogged by trouble from the first days of its existence: the business failures of 1873; defeat by the Church over control of education; the attempted assassination of Wilhelm I; the badly miscarried attempt to repress the Socialists by law; the deaths, in immediate succession, of Wilhelm I and Friedrich III. And eighteen years after the time described, nearly at the end of this unlucky author's unfortunate life, a series of episodes like something out of *Hamlet*: a German Kaiser nearly dying in the streets, saved only by a passing droshky driver, who tears the blocked cannula that is suffocating him out of his throat; the new Kaiser beginning his reign with the arrest of his own mother; and, finally, the funeral of Wilhelm I, at which the adjutant carrying the flag in front of the casket is completely drunk, and has to be supported as he walks, while Bismarck, in the procession that follows, wears a blonde wig to protect his bald head in his fear of catching cold, that Arctic day in June. This is how it is when the gods, insulted, retaliate.

As Hamlet says: 'It is not, nor it cannot come to good.'

While at Prien, I visited an old, old man who lived there, and who as a very young man served as a footman at the court of Ludwig II just before catastrophe struck that monarch. Strangely, and like all those I have ever met who were in immediate contact with the King, the man cannot be dissuaded from the notion that Ludwig II was not at all mentally ill, but was rather the innocent victim of a plot originating in Berlin. He claims that he was present during a heated argument between two doctors at Schloss Berg, when each of the two medical men in attendance accused the other of having falsified the psychiatric diagnosis. I do not want to take a position on this one way or the other, but I have for years wondered about the inexplicable animosity evinced by the physician Gudden in his handling of the case at the time – the same Gudden who months before the catastrophe had allowed his colleagues' malicious comments about the King to stand unchallenged, and who, after Ludwig II had been confined, could not conceal a certain satisfaction about the outcome: as though it gave him a feeling of power to be the psychiatrist who had put away a king.

Furthermore, the genes which were causative factors in the development of the psychoses of King Ludwig and King Otto were not at all, as the north Germans delight in believing, the result of intermarriage between and among Habsburgs and Wittelsbachs, with the resulting defects of inbreeding. On the contrary, the defective characteristics were derived from the disease which the grandfather of both kings, Prince Wilhelm the Elder of Prussia, brought back from the Wars of Liberation, and which he then passed on to both his grandsons through his daughter, Queen Marie of Bavaria, in the form of defective germ-cell structure.

This is, therefore, most definitely not a Bavarian product, but something which was imported from Berlin. Furthermore, mentally ill or not, there is not another monarch in modern European history who lives on from beyond the grave as does Ludwig II. Just as in 1918, in the midst of the Revolution, people believed he had returned, so today, legend has it – and not only that of peasants – that he can be seen on winter nights, rushing through the snows of the Wettersteingebirge in a ghostly sleigh.

Along these lines, I, who have seen death enter the circle of my friends much too often in recent years, have an experience of my own to relate. It concerns my house, a very isolated place more than six hundred years old, which has long been regarded as haunted, and has its ghostly monk, who is supposed to fly over the river and appear at the windows of the dining-room.

I, of course, have never seen him. I have observed that there are strange sounds in my house, on occasion the heavy rolling of something like a bowling ball; that the light suddenly goes on in the middle of the night; and that for no earthly reason the door to my bedroom will suddenly open. I have put all this down, as one customarily does, to the nightly prowling of cats, to a loose electrical contact, to a worn-out door lock, and have never been too greatly concerned about these manifestations.

Lately, however, my household has been upset by something new, and of a far less common nature. Since last autumn, since the time death struck so deep into my life, we have all, independently of one another, noticed that in the attic room which has always been considered the starting point for these ghostly episodes, there is a hideous smell of decomposition. And the smell is not restricted to this room either, but drifts about the whole house, disappears above, suddenly reappears on the ground floor, and then is perceptible on the second floor. This cannot possibly be a matter of suggestion, since we have had guests from Munich who had no idea of all this, and yet a minute after they had entered their rooms reappeared to tell us that there was a penetrating odour of something rotting in their bedrooms.

Naturally, our first thought was of dead mice in the mattresses, or even under the floorboards. Naturally, we made the most thorough examination without finding a thing. And here is the most incredible part: at this point, the odour began positively to mock us, moving from place to place in a single room in some inexplicable way. It now no longer filled the whole room, but seemed to spring from one article or piece of furniture to the next, now on a chair, then to some easily overlooked point like a light bulb, after which it might disappear from there and turn up again abruptly on the bow of my cello. We could find nothing and had to put up with the thing. Then, as the yearly mass for my dead friends was being said, the phenomenon observed and confirmed by a total of ten persons completely disappeared. I tell all this knowing I run the risk of being laughed at by all kinds of intellectuals with horn-rimmed eyeglasses.

Further, there is the matter of my friend Gwosdinski, whose house was destroyed, roof to basement, in an air-raid. He writes me that several days before the catastrophe his cat was transformed from a young and kittenish creature beloved by all to a completely different kind of animal which hung its head and whined constantly for no apparent reason. The night of the bombing, the cat was rescued, but it tore itself away and as though hypnotised by something it saw in the flames ran back into the building. Its body was not found in the ruins. Again, I merely cite the fact, without either affirming or denying. But I myself recently had an experience which seems to me to deny explanation without making use of the transcendental.

When I was a young man, the great conservative, von Heydebrandt, a colleague of my father's in the Reichstag, had taken some notice of me. In the autumn of 1918, he retired from the political arena, and I lost sight of him, and did not think of him again until a night in October 1924, when I dreamed that he had died. Several days later, I learned that he had passed away.

As to Herr Hitler again, there is suddenly in my mind his laying the corner-stone for the Haus der Deutschen Kunst. He was handed a hammer with which to strike the three traditional blows. But as he raised his arm the head of the hammer flew off the end of the handle, and spun so far away that it could no longer be found in the confusion of the crowd. I could see how deeply that superstitious hysteric was affected by the omen.

His opponents took this as a good sign, and we hoped at the time that the regime might soon collapse. We have now been waiting for more than ten years. Our hair has been made gray by grief and sorrow, we have poisoned ourselves with a deadly and irreconcilable hatred which makes us prefer death to giving up the hope of seeing our enemy destroyed. We have held to the right, and have not surrendered, at the sacrifice of the best years of our lives. And now, in our hatred, we are like bees who must pay with their lives for the use of their stingers.

And yet, is there one of us who would have chosen peace and prosperity under Hitler, knowing as we do that such a life can only be founded on tears, and robbery, and murder? I know of none! I only know people among my friends and fellow fighters who will never be reconciled – I only know people who would ten times rather die than bear the triumph of this monster. I only know people who would rather weep with God than laugh with Satan!

But it is over now, the laughing, and he knows it. The end is at hand – not a heroic but a dirty end, in shame and degradation and the mocking laughter of the rest of the world! It does sometimes happen that a would-be great man is allowed to toy with the levers of the gigantic machinery of history. This goes on for some time, and the fool is not destroyed. But suddenly the wheels begin to move, faster and faster, and he is thrown into the machinery and crushed. Stalingrad: ever since, *He* has been going about in a condition the French call 'cul nu', and a new expression is spreading among the people, more damaging than any propaganda from the regime has ever been: '*Gröfaz*'. That is now his nickname, *Gröfaz*, an abbreviation of 'Greatest Field Marshal of All Time': *Gröfaz*. A miserable hysteric may play Alexander the Great before the world for a while. But sooner or later, history comes along and tears the mask off his face.

Gröfaz....

March 1943

The monster has been given the evil tidings of Stalingrad. Naturally, it is going to raise itself for one last blow. And so terror has been loosed among us, once more.

Himmler: I met him just once, at a party marking the New Year of 1934, after Clé and I had been whirled through the confusion to land among these rather questionable people. At this point, this individual of strongly middle-class antecedents and the appearance of a bailiff felt called upon to drag me off to a corner and ask me who Herr Arno Rechberg was.

Since Herr Rechberg, an extremely wealthy man and a high-ranking Mason, played one of the key roles in the fall of von Seeckt and in bringing about the Conference of Locarno, and was, in addition, one of the figures behind the scenes at the Herrenklub and in the cabinet of von Papen, and since I knew him only casually, I attempted to extricate myself from the situation by answering Himmler's question with another question: How did it happen, I asked, that the Fouché of the Third Reich had to turn for information about such a personage to poor me?

He looked at me in surprise out of his short-sighted eyes. I believe that my dialectical parry was lost on him for the simple reason that he did not know who Fouché was. But, not wanting to appear ignorant, he let me alone.

I was very glad to get rid of him. This air of the subaltern he had about him, and the ineffaceable stamp of the *petit bourgeois* – in combination with his absolute power to kill anyone – were precisely what made him so frightful. This must have been the way

Fouquier-Tinville looked: the rigid bureaucrat, Minister in Charge of the Underworld.

This is the man now slowly elbowing his way to the front. And this is how we live now, as people must have lived before Thermidor and the overthrow of Robespierre – underground and essentially illegally, open at any moment to denunciation and the executioner's axe. The Summary Courts, presided over by sadistic and bloodthirsty Nazi Jacobins, make quick work of sentencing people to death, and five-minute trials suffice. Stamped on the verdict order are the words 'Liquidate and Expropriate' – which means execution and seizure of all property. The victim is shoved out a back door, where the executioner already awaits him. In fifteen minutes it is all over, trial, sentencing, everything. Next comes the towering guillotine, and in university dissecting rooms the cadavers of the decapitated are piling up so high that university officials have refused further shipments of these silent guests.

Heads roll for a bagatelle: they roll for doubts about the outcome of a war which anyone with half an eye knew was lost long ago. They roll for holding back a pound note, and they roll especially fast because of aspersions cast on the Great General – as though one could cast aspersions on Caesar sitting there atop the Obersalzberg, who last year in the presence of someone I know called himself the present-day 'Scipio Africanus', and who falls into a paroxysm of rage if someone dares to doubt his affinity with God! As Lord High Executioner, he has converted the punishment for 'causing ridicule of the Führer' from the former six-week jail sentence into death by beheading. And we now have, as I am informed by the Traunstein public prosecutor, eleven guillotines in Germany. Recently, when the one in Munich went out of order, the Stuttgart guillotine was borrowed to help out.

But production has never been better. A Palatinate man was beheaded because he pleaded with his only son not to take unnecessary risks at the Front. A 74-year-old bank director from Stuttgart was beheaded because he was overheard on a train talking to another old man about the fact that the war was going badly.... Oh, and they have even cruelly cut off the head of one of the two whorehouse madams in the employ of Herr Christian Weber, that owner of two bordellos and bosom friend of the Greatest General of All Time, the whole crime of this worthy lady being that, probably at the behest of her employer, she had asked for foreign currency in payment for the fleshly pleasures offered, and also that she had withheld for herself a small percentage of each day's receipts.

Estimates are that in Berlin alone there are sixteen beheadings a week, while in Vienna, where hatred of the Prussians is now white-hot, the figure is twenty a week. The hangman has two *jours fixes* per week, on which he works on a mass-production basis. Since he receives a commission for each hanging, plus his regular salary from the government, he obviously has a stake in the enterprise. I can imagine a notice in the 'Personals' column of a newspaper, composed in the proper New German proportions of sentimentality and sadism, reading something like this:

GOVERNMENT OFFICIAL

Military man, in well-paid, pension-covered position, tall, blond, good appearance, nature-lover with definite views on life, seeks correspondence with like-minded woman, also blonde, with view to marriage. Not less than 5'2"and not over 25.

Gentleman prefers blondes. *Non olet:* these platinum-blonde Ingrids, Wibkes, Astrids, Gudruns, and Isoldes would never hold their noses at hubby's profession. After all, this is vital government work. You think I exaggerate the hangman's social acceptability? Let me cite the following case, an episode of recent occurrence in Vienna:

The well-known actress, M., a lady who was a leading tragedienne during the heyday of the Burgtheater and then became owner of a wine-making establishment, from time to time had to dinner an official whose black market connections were of use on occasion. One day, this official brought with him to dinner an 'acquaintance' who was extremely taciturn, seemed almost to avoid human contact, would not look one in the eye, and when asked if he was a resident of Vienna, replied in north German dialect that he maintained no regular residence, but had business in Vienna rather often. Afterwards, when the man had left, the lady learned that her guest at table that evening had been the hangman, in person....

On the same subject, while in Munich recently, I was a spectator at a Summary Court trial, and saw a 65-year-old doctor convicted for possession of foreign currency sentenced to a mere eight years in prison, although he missed the guillotine by a hair. The courtroom, a low-ceilinged, ill-lit and musty-smelling place, on the smoke-streaked wall of which a photograph of the old Regent, left hanging by some oversight, looked on as though through a window of another world; the defendant, a trembling and stuttering old man; and the denouncer and chief prosecution witness, a sleek, blonde floozy – Swiss, incidentally – who had been the old man's housekeeper; the assistant judges, two civil servants; and the chief judge, pinched-faced, resentment in every line, a beast, a piece of filth, a Nazi horror who had climbed out of a fathomless depth in Lower Bavaria somewhere....

No, this man's name was not Fuchs[59], who sent the Scholls, brother and sister, to the guillotine a few days ago, and whom we will soon drag before *our* tribunal. This man was called Rossdorfer, and he was until yesterday a counsel-at-law in the town of Plattling. Now, this canaille was getting a chance to vent the accumulation of decades of hatred of the 'professors', and this unlucky old doctor denounced by this Swiss harlot was a made-to-order target. The trial itself couldn't have been faster, the blonde nearly burst with National Socialist loyalty as she reiterated her denunciation; the old man tried to stutter something in defence, but the Lord High Judge roared him down before he could get out three words. The two assistant judges, who recognised me and were ashamed, avoided my somewhat ironical glance and, to give the appearance of legality to what they were doing, asked a couple of questions meant to be objective. The old fellow sensed a change in the air, took courage in hand and began to speak – and was at once given the knockout blow by a frightful intermezzo....

What happened was that our wise and just judge, previously composer of grammatically questionable briefs for knife-wielding peasants and tax-evading pedlars, suddenly roared out the word 'Baloney', banged his files down on the table and, purple with rage, engulfed the old man in bellowing. And then he did something which must be unprecedented in jurisprudence. He leaped from his chair, ran over to the old man, and shaking his fist under his nose, roared: 'Listen, you! If you keep on with this stuff, I'll punch you one in the snoot!'

At which the taking of evidence was concluded, and the accused was ready for sentencing. He was given eight years, at his age very likely tantamount to a death sentence.

I left, thinking of many things: of that English parliamentary tribunal whose awe and respect for the brilliance of the crown once worn by Charles Stuart, and for the suffering of a man about to die, was such that it sent him to the block with something like a guard of honour; of that much maligned French tribunal which granted the condemned Charlotte Corday her request for an artist to paint her portrait before she was hanged, because the murderess of Marat wished to leave 'an example and a warning' to posterity. This happened exactly 150 years ago, almost to the day, and the world has not only gone to the dogs in the interim, but several degrees worse: it has gone to the likes of this fastidious gentleman, who takes evidence with the aid of his manly fist, and will give the defendant, if he does not confess, 'one in the snoot'.

I ponder all this as I move heavily about Munich, observing how badly wounded it was in the last air-raid – this city which was once so gay and beautiful. And at just this moment, I learn for the first time of the martyrdom of the Scholls.

I never saw these two young people. In my rural isolation, I got only bits and pieces of the whole story of what they were doing, but the significance of what I heard was such I could hardly believe it. The Scholls are the first in Germany to have had the courage to witness for the truth. The movement they left at their deaths will go on, and as is always the case with martyrdom, they have sown seeds which will raise important fruit in time to come. This young brother and sister went boldly about their work, almost as though they were defying death. Their betrayal came through a miserable university proctor, who was then so afraid of being beaten or otherwise punished, that he had to be taken into protective custody.

They were sentenced to death by a second example of the Rossdorfer-type. They died in all the radiance of their courage and readiness for sacrifice, and thereby attained the pinnacle in lives well lived.

I have learned something of their background from the young people who were with them. These were children who stood apart from the rest, of good Swabian stock, living in quiet, almost cloistered isolation, but even then having about them that special aura which presages early death. Their bearing before the tribunal – that of the girl, especially – was inspiring. They flung their contempt of the court, the Party, and that insane, would-be great man, Hitler, into the faces of their judges, and at the end, did something which carries the icy breath of the Eternal about it for us who survive. For, with their last words, they repeated the warning once given by the condemned Knights of the Temple to their judges, that those who were persecuting them and those who stood behind them would 'within a year be called to judgement before the throne of God'. The curse pronounced by the Templars was realised to the extent that before a year was past both Pope Clemens V and King Philip IV of France were dead. It remains to be seen what will happen here in the course of the next year....

But the Scholls departed from this life quietly, and gravely and with wonderful dignity gave their young blood. On their grave-stones let these words be carved, and let this entire people, which has lived in deepest degradation these last ten years, blush when it reads them: '*Cogi non potest quisquis mori scit*' – He who knows how to die can never be enslaved.

We will all of us, someday, have to make a pilgrimage to their graves, and stand before them, ashamed.

This is the story of these two children of our race: the latest, and God willing, the *first* Germans of a great rebirth of the spirit.

But Herr Hitler is occupied elsewhere at the moment; Herr Hitler is concerned, now while our cathedrals and national monuments are being turned into dust, with the teaching of counterpoint and the rules of harmony – Herr Hitler is laying the foundations of National Socialist music. And recently, Herr Göring was seen entering a party he was giving for his cronies wearing a fur coat that reached to his ankles, girdled by a red morocco belt studded with stolen diamonds, and with red morocco boots on his feet. I am sure he looked grand – this field marshal who never commanded in battle. But there is a precedent here in history: that unlucky Roman, Caligula, also appeared before his gaping subjects in red morocco boots, shortly before he became unmistakably insane.

August 1943

I found Kleeblatt,[60] my doctor, grieving over the death by the guillotine of his stepson, who wrote the leaflets distributed by the Scholls, and was beheaded with those two youthful martyrs: with great effort, he had managed to forestall the corpse's being dismembered and put into bottles of Lysol in anatomy classes.

But the ghosts of the dead have begun their work, and already the effects are felt in the systematic demoralisation of the Nazi ruling structure. For weeks now, the lower echelons of hierarchy, district officials, township leaders, and bastions of the regime generally have been making gestures, meant to be noticed, of disillusionment with the Nazis. Their general demeanour is now supposed to convey disgust, so that everybody may know their dissatisfaction, their unhappiness about the present state of things. Now, in the post office, for instance, the clerk is liable to fling official notices contemptuously to one side, muttering that he has 'had enough of this swindle'.

The secret behind this transformation? All these gentlemen have in recent days received a letter from a certain 'revolutionary executive', informing them that they will be held responsible for their official actions; that previous denunciations and similar crimes have been duly recorded against them, and that the continuation of such activities will further worsen the consequences for them. By great good luck, I got hold of one of these missives:

We possess documentary evidence regarding your activities since 1933, and you will be held responsible for them following the collapse of Hitlerism. The Executive Committee hereby informs you that you will henceforth remain under the most intensive observation. If there should occur a single further instance of activity on behalf of the present regime, or if any additional reports are confirmed of harm done to political opponents, the sentence of death which has been pronounced against you for future execution will be extended to include your entire family. Execution will be by hanging on the day of overthrow of the regime.

It had its effect. These letters were in some incomprehensible way sent registered mail from widely separated places, so that those sent to Bavaria originated in Insterburg, while the letters mailed to East Prussia evidently came from Baden or Württemberg.

In any case, the effect was salutary. The minor satraps have simply stopped functioning, schoolteachers are once again to be seen in church, the women's leader has quieted down, and the local 'Party bastion' gets ill with unfailing punctuality when called upon to hold a meeting. I drove into Munich with the wife of a Trostberg doctor, who told me that in 1938, her husband, then head of the local medical organisation, had stopped treating Jews – including accident cases. Now, the woman related, her husband had trouble with his nerves, complained constantly about the purposelessness of life and the unreality of the Party pronouncements, and was even toying with ideas of suicide. And why? Because one of these mysterious Executive Committees had sentenced him to be removed from the medical rolls for 'inhumane conduct unbecoming to a physician', effective 'the day of the overthrow' when the sentence 'might be supplemented by further punishment'.

Incidentally, the couriers who carried these letters halfway across Germany risked their lives on every trip.

The day before yesterday, W., who is the leader of this organisation of students, artists, and intellectuals, came to my house: a man deeply embittered by the death of his soldier son; sixty-three years old, with the elasticity of one in his thirties, and a face so haggard it is the very picture of death. And so I have been enrolled in a phalanx whose members' lives are from now on balanced on a razor's edge.

We talked through the whole of a midsummer night and well into the bright morning – about future propagandising, about the English radio broadcasts (unfortunately so often misinformed about the trend of German public opinion), about points to be added to our program in future.

Herewith, a small sampling:

Immediate and definitive elimination of Berlin and Prussia as political centres of gravity.

An organisation to be launched at once, which will take over the task of cleansing the area of southern Germany immediately upon the overthrow of the Nazis.

Immediate expulsion of all Prussians arrived here since 1920. Immediate destruction of all war industry established in Bavaria since 1933.

Further, in order to ensure the emergence of a new Germany: immediate and complete expropriation of all heavy industry; immediate nationalisation of factories; immediate indictment for high treason for all those who have joined in dividing the spoils of the Hitler regime, with the very first trials to be of the von Papens, Meissners, Neuraths, Hindenburgs, Schröters, and their like.

Immediate indictment of all the generals responsible for the continuance of the war.

Not a bad beginning; not entirely devoid of hyperbole, certainly, and yet not without its germs of ideas as to how to end the mistakes of the last eighty years.

And are we bad Germans because we deliberate these things? This depends on which Germany you mean. If by 'Germany' is meant that gigantic heresy of Bismarck's which is today in extremis, if it is forgotten that before that there existed a Reich which was the cradle and focus of the great ideas, and that this

Reich lasted a thousand years, while the newcomers from Potsdam lasted a few decades before they failed, dragging down with them into the dust all the cultural treasures, the irreplaceable artefacts, the very memory of that earlier thousand years – then we are bad Germans!

No, we are pondering these things because the future cannot be jerrybuilt. If we again botch things as we did in 1919, our grandchildren will shed their blood in still another Prussian-sponsored slaughter. Paradoxical as it may sound, we will have won the war if we can release Germany from Prussian hegemony, lift off its mercantilist superstructure, and free it of the senseless over-industrialisation possible only because the government subsidises it. This is the only way we will ever remove the purposeless and, in the highest sense, unproductive human ballast we now must carry, even if the job of removal takes decades. And this is also the only way we will be sure that if we have not won, at least, I.G. Farben has *lost* the war.

20 August 1943

An English leaflet reproaches the *Schwarze Korps* for locating the basis of all wars not in the actions of men but in the subterranean machinations of demons, and the English attack the magazine for ascribing these catastrophes to irrational causes. Now I am not to be listed among the apologists for *Schwarze Korps*, or for Gunter d'Alquen – whose real name is probably Gunter Schulze. I would be the first to grant that the very real, flesh-and-blood individuals responsible for this war – the company directors greedy for bigger profits, the Army generals greedy for more medals, the street-corner bums greedy for more balm for their egos, who have now been promoted to politician status – have been exposed this time as perhaps never before in a war.

But having said this, have we resolved the problem? Have we explained the lethargy, the almost frenzied lack of consistency of the masses in accepting Hitler just five years after having declared themselves generally pacifist, in the elections of May 1928? Have we explained the behaviour of the females who, as I described earlier, were so overcome by the sight of Hitler they swallowed the gravel he had walked on? Does the behaviour of that Hitler Youth boy who threw a crucifix out of the window, yelling, 'Lie there, you Jew pig!' thereby become more explicable – or the ethical demoralisation, the brutalising, the appetite for murder of the younger generation? And do people in England really think that all of this was possible without the emergence from out of the night of a form of delirium that could very well tomorrow seize hold of any other people?

I must admit that the whole argument depresses me. It shows the gulf that exists between continental European and Atlantic – or insular – thinking on the subject. They are still trying to come to terms with this historical ghost story by using the old, worn-out formulas of the nineteenth century.

Certainly, we are going to sit in judgement on the visible individuals who pulled the strings here, certainly the wood for the gallows on which I hope to see Hitler, Göring, Goebbels, Papen, *et al.*, hung has already been thoughtfully put aside. And certainly, too, all of us Germans will have to take our Cross upon our backs and carry it through the dark Valley of Sorrow before the Absolute is attained.

But is there a nation today so lacking in perspective as to deny the possibility that such a mass psychosis could at some time in its history occur within its own boundaries? Do people really go so far as to accuse unarmed German intellectuals of lethargy when, during the first two years of the Hitler regime, at least, the British Cabinet, with every possible weapon at its disposal, was itself too indolent to smoke the brown rats out of their holes?

I am not even complaining that the old game of who-is-really-guilty is being played here. What disturbs me is the methodology of this kind of thinking, which overlooks the real problem and in mindless and so-comfortable shutting of the eyes refuses to face the great crisis of our time. Woe to the nation which does not hear the thunder of the apocalyptic hoofs! Woe to any people under the sun of Satan, who do not learn now, as this sun makes its terrible ascent, to believe in God! Woe to the folk who are incapable of absorbing this single fact:

Rationalism has had its day. That heresy ruled the world for 400 years, and now its time is past. The Great Mystery, the irrational itself, is again knocking at the door. Today, I witnessed the first air-attack by American planes, a bombing in broad daylight of Regensburg. It was my first personal and really close contact with the war. There they flew, over my quiet valley, these snow-white birds.... I saw one, hit by anti-aircraft, glow dark red a moment, and then fall in a shroud of flames. I saw tiny figures in their parachutes detach themselves from the flames, and then I saw the cords of one of the chutes catch fire and the human load depending on it plunge to the ground. I drove to Seebruck to look at the wreckage. Burning oil bubbled in a crater fourteen feet deep at the wreckage. The engines had bored so deeply into the ground that no attempt was being made to dig them out. Around the crater, pieces of the human body were scattered – a foot, a finger, an arm. The remains were carried off in a small potato sack.

Near W., a couple of Americans were luckier and landed safely. But then, as they were being led off, two refugees tried to spit at them, and only the fact that the soldier escorting the Americans declared that he would not allow it and waved his gun as a warning saved these defenceless men from this indignity. You really have only to scratch your average non-bourgeois to find underneath that good old substance of human decency and that inborn aversion to the actions of canaille.

The news from Hamburg is simply beyond the grasp of the imagination – streets of boiling asphalt into which the victims sank and were boiled alive, veritable cities of ruins, which cover the dead and surround those still alive like some jagged stone martyr's crown. The talk is of 200,000 dead.

I am not one who believes everything he is told. I much prefer seeing the thing for myself. And I think that in this case what I have seen with my own eyes suffices.

I have heard a great deal about the completely wild and disoriented behaviour of people in Hamburg as the city burned, stories of amnesia, stories of people wandering through the streets in the pyjamas they had on when they fled from their houses, crazy-eyed, carrying an empty bird cage, with no memory of a yesterday, and no idea of a tomorrow.

And now this is what I saw on a burning-hot day in early August at a little railroad station in Upper Bavaria, where forty or fifty of these miserable people were milling about, scrambling, despite the angry roars of the station-master, into a car through a window they had broken, pushing, kicking, yelling, accustomed by now to fighting for space.

What happened then was inevitable. A suitcase, a miserable lump of cardboard with edges broken off, missed the target, fell back to the platform and broke open, revealing its contents. There was a pile of clothes, a manicure kit, a toy. And there was the baked corpse of a child, shrunk to the proportions of a mummy, which the half-crazed woman had dragged along with her, the macabre remains of what only a few days before had been a family. Cries of dismay, disgust, roars, hysterical outbursts, the snarls of a small dog, until finally an official took pity on all of them and had the thing disposed of.

Another report I heard was that the fire-storm created by the immense conflagration sucked up into it all the oxygen, suffocating people who were far away from the actual flames, and that the rain of phosphorus broiled the corpses of grown men and women into tiny, child-sized mummies, so that countless women are now wandering about the country, their homes in ruins, carrying with them these ghastly relics.

In the face of this, can it still be denied that with this war an epoch is reaching its end? Can the fact still be blinked away that technology is playing out its last grim moments, and that it is leaving behind a dreadful vacuum of soul-emptiness – a vacuum which can probably only be filled by something antirational, antimechanical, an 'x reaction' compounded of newly risen demons? Is there any doubt that there is no possible way anymore back to the world of yesterday, and that this time those riders now saddling their black steeds are none other than the Four Horsemen of the Apocalypse themselves?

2 July 1944

Today, bicycling home from Stein, I came upon a mob of youthful female factory workers. All from northern Germany, evacuated here and 'allocated' – to use one of the lovely terms of the new business-German – to the Alz Valley's chemical plants. They were close packed as a heap of mussels, like all this nation, and marching in military formation. The effect was as ugly, as irritating, as devoid of everything feminine as the BDM itself. They trotted by like a herd of cows with blonde tail-braids, and I shall have to explain why I found them even important enough to go on about....

It is because of the song they were singing. The song was one of those things with a choppy rhythm borrowed from the Bolsheviks by our musical purveyors-to-the-court: insignificant trash, in short. But the refrain is worth noting:

> Where the flames leap
> From the opera house
> Is my hometown,
> Is my native house.

Now, you will admit that for people who are being bombed that is a remarkable song! A query brought the information that these bovine figures with their lymphatic faces were from Hannover, where the opera house really did go up in flames. I would not dare to say whether what is involved here is opposition, self-derision, protest, or merely more of the general cow-likeness into which the Nazis have turned German women. Probably it is just one more example of the general state of idiocy here.

I must add something from a conversation at the Traunstein railroad station with two members of the Berlin Philharmonic I know. These two, who have retained, naturally, their mental agility and their angry protest, told me about an amusing variation to the customary form of the daily Army communiqué, as this is whispered about in Munich:

Bulletin from the perplexed Army post: from the upholsterer's headquarters:

The latest Army communiqué does not yet lie around.[61]

Very good, certainly, very good. Of course, I would prefer seeing resistance to the regime take the form of partisan-group organisation rather than these more or less funny jokes. At best, these things mirror the isolation, the cowardice, and the lethargy which the Nazis have set in motion here with their complete castration of the German people.

I should note, to be quite fair, that I have heard of a Bavarian band of partisans operating around Murnau and an Austrian group around St Johann, in the Pinzgau. These groups are composed, naturally, of Army deserters and of workers who have left their jobs – but how much sorrow we could have spared the world if we had started this kind of thing earlier!

And thus I come back to the puzzle which has been troubling me for eleven years, the old puzzle of the German mass psychosis, of the generals who allow themselves to be physically manhandled by Herr Hitler (and what does a man of sixty-five years of age have left to lose that is so very important except his dignity?) – without striking down this 'gentleman' out of a furnished room on Munich's Barerstrasse; of the hysterical females who are his fanatical supporters; I come back to the problem represented by children like the eleven-year-old Gregor Srasser, who watched his father being murdered by order of Herr Hitler in the summer of

1934, and then, just four weeks after the murder, explained: 'The Führer did it, and what the Führer does is right.'

Ah, gigantic psychosis, drunkenness on a mass scale beyond measuring, which will be followed by the most horrible morning-after the world has ever known! Here, here is the product of your radio manipulation – stupefied mass-man, and the conversion of human societies into heaps of termites! And with this have gone the discouragement and final silencing of the real intelligentsia, a factor not to be overlooked, and, following, the creation of a mob which I, who have seen the United States and know something about Soviet Russia also – although the latter is hardly to be mentioned in this connection – declare to be the most infernal human dregs in the world today.

It should be noted that the people I am talking about are not of proletarian origins. These are derived from the middle-class – lower-rank officials, elementary schoolteachers, postal officials part way up the scale. They come from that infernal class Sombart described as the 'shackle on all true progress', a citation I read in *Revolt of the Masses* by Ortega y Gasset, which is rather frowned upon in today's Germany because of the cosmopolitan, Girondist spirit it breathes.

I think that those of us who are now gathering the materials for a written history of the Third Reich will be obliged, when we have combined it all into a single work, to call it *The Revolt of the Mailmen and the Schoolteachers*.

18 July 1944

From my Chiemgau house, I saw the worst bombing ever of Munich. For three solid hours, the drone never stopped, and a never-ceasing thunder of exploding bombs shook the earth. And even here, ninety kilometres away, the air pressure shattered windows. Then the powerful drone of the propellers roared overhead. Quite near, I heard two detonations, presumably the firing of anti-aircraft. I saw one of these silver metal birds – I don't know whether it was German or English – spiral down in a long glide to the earth, like a leaf made tired by the coming of autumn. It fell about five or ten kilometres from here.

Who is going to vouch that some other bomber will not fall through my roof, so that this little property of mine, so bitterly fought for, rescued with difficulty from the time of inflation, is not destroyed? A recent English broadcast named Hörpolding as the site of the munition depot. Hörpolding is just eight kilometres from here, in line of flight. Also, the whole lower valley of my clear and guiltless river has been contaminated by the industrial plague brought here by the generals who are mainly responsible for the destruction of Germany.

I look at the things I have brought together here, and cherish, the library, the medieval statuettes, the candelabra from the Middle Ages, the drawings, and it seems to me often now that these things have a strangeness about them, and I want to cry. Ah, have you ever looked about you at the possessions of a man on his deathbed, knowing that all of it would soon be scattered to the four winds?

An endless stream of refugees is now moving down the nearby autobahn, heading away from Munich, where tens of thousands of bombed-out people have spent rainy nights camped in the streets off the Maximiliansplatz – broken old women with long sticks on their shoulders to which are attached bundles containing all they own in the world, miserable, homeless people, with burned clothes, in whose eyes there is still the horror of the fire-storm, the pulverising explosions, the burial under debris, the frightful death in the cellars where people suffocated amidst the river of sewage and excreta from the burst mains.

But why should Herr Hitler worry, as, we are told, in his shelter being dug constantly deeper into the earth, he reads a novel a day, and at night – restless, painful nights of the mass murderer and sentimental gangster – spends his time watching movies? Why should that lout named Speer worry, either, with that clean-cut expression of his, which is the epitome of this whole sickening, mechanical, little-boy-at-heart generation? I must admit something about Speer: after Papen, who combines the conscience and sense of honour of a butcher's hound with stupidity so devastating it is not an excuse but a crime, and just after these new-German pseudo-Girondists and ersatz aristocrats of the type of Krupp *et al.*, his is the most sickening face I know among Nazidom's second string – and he imagines himself to be the reincarnation of Leonardo da Vinci.

20 July 1944

Maria Olczewska[62] has come for a visit. We talked about Furtwängler – a subject I hardly want to touch on. There is, evidently, a way of conducting in a 'blonde' manner. And the favouring of this shade, whether in fact or as a concept, is something which in itself compromises the man who does it.

I can't help it.

21 July 1944

And now the attempt to assassinate Hitler. Carried out by the Count von Stauffenberg whose irreproachable father I have always considered to be one of the last remaining examples of the true German nobleman. Behind it – a revolt of the generals, long awaited.

Ah, now, really, gentlemen, this is a little late. You made this monster, and as long as things were going well you gave him whatever he wanted. You turned Germany over to this arch-criminal, you swore allegiance to him by every incredible oath he chose to put before you – you, officers of the Crown, all of you. And so you made yourselves into the Mamelukes of a man who carries on his head responsibility for a hundred thousand murders and who is the cause of the sorrow and the object of the curses of the whole of the world.

And now you are betraying him, as yesterday you betrayed the Republic, and as the day before yesterday you betrayed the Monarchy. Oh, I don't doubt that if this coup had succeeded, we, and what remains of the material substance of this country, would have been saved. I am sorry, the whole of this nation is sorry, that you failed.

But then to think that you, who are the embodiment of the Prussian heresy, that sower of evil, that stench in the nostrils of humanity – that you may be Germany's future leaders? No.

I am a conservative. In Germany, naturally, this is an almost extinct political species. I derive from monarchical patterns of thinking, I was brought up as a monarchist, and the continued existence of the monarchy is one of the foundation stones of my physical well-being. And yet – not *despite* this fact, but *because* of it – I hate you. Coquettes who flirt with every passing political adventurer! Renegades, betrayers of your past! Miserable bed-fellows of that same industrial oligarchy with whose coming to power commenced the destruction of our societal and govern-mental structure! Obedient planners of the attempt, now gone awry, at burglarising Russia, under the aegis of Krupp & Co., the very planning of which only reveals your political dilettantism and geopolitical ignorance! Men who have left the realm of all propriety and order! Unconscionable advocates of every conceiv-able form of godlessness and soullessness – haters of the beautiful and everything which excludes your flat Prussian utilitarianism!

Prince Rupprecht told me how, years ago, as an Army commander in the First World War, he pleaded with Ludendorff to spare the castle of Coucy, a priceless architectural treasure which lay between the opposing armies. 'It was really of no military value, either to us or to the enemy. Neither side had ever attempted to use it for military purposes. But the fact that I advocated sparing it, and that I feared that destruction of the castle would only mean a blow to our prestige, quite uselessly – this brought Coucy to Ludendorff's attention. He prevailed, and the castle was destroyed, if for no better reason than to strike at me.

'But he did not hate that castle just because I wanted to preserve it. He hated Coucy because he hated everything which lay outside his barracks view of life – spirit, taste, elegance, everything that gives distinction to life.'

Ah, this unworthy nephew of great Moltke and all his caste could hardly be better described. For years, these men were the cover for every treasonable act, every orgy of rape and murder, because Hitler allowed them prominence once again in a debased, Prussianised Germany. They defended him, verbally and physically, every time he committed one of his criminal acts, they went blithely on past the suffering of all the bombing victims, the prisoners in the concentration camps, and the religious persecutors, and they hummed a little tune to words like 'Germany' or the 'German spirit', because a different regime would have meant the end of their power....

And now that the firm is going bankrupt, they are betraying it to provide themselves with a political alibi – just as they betrayed all the others who were no longer useful in their drive to get and hold power.

The nation mourns the fact that this bomb did not explode where and when it should have, and I cannot possibly express how deeply I share everyone's feeling. But as to the generals: as soon as Germany is liberated from the Prussian heresy, they should be killed, along with the industrialists who launched this war, and their journalist bards, and the Messrs Meissner and Hindenburg Jr and, let us not forget, the whole of that crew responsible for the immense misdeed of 30 January 1933, who ought to be hanged twenty feet higher than the rest. And let the ones who are spared be condemned to spend the rest of their lives selling matches and wastepaper, living caricatures to remind us of how and by whom power was once stolen to bring endless sorrow down on our heads.

I can't help it.

16 August 1944

The air reeks of death. I am not referring here, even, to what is broadcast from abroad – that 5,000 officers have been shot; that the Nazis are murdering everybody not to their liking regardless of whether there is a connection with the assassination attempt – yes, and shooting the family of the suspect at the same time they execute him to finish the job.

No, what I have in mind is something that surrounds us like a frightful presage of things to come, that fills the summer air, and gives a ghostly cast to the light of the sun, so that it is as though we live day and night in the glare of a huge funeral torch. It is the certainty of approaching catastrophe that fills all our minds, horror and the horror of death that surround us. What is to become of a thoroughly coarsened people who instil in their youths the idea that political burglary and the murder of whole peoples are entirely legitimate life-aims, and whose military leaders did not for a single moment hesitate to back everything that was done, as long as things seemed to be going well.

We breathe the air of death. We do not need to be told so, as the Woman's Organisation leader in Obing, a harmless farm village, told us recently, when she extolled this 'Führer' of ours because 'in his goodness, he has prepared a gentle and easy death by gas for the German people in case the war ends badly.' Oh, I am not writing fiction. This lovely lady is no creature of my imagination. I saw her with my own eyes: a golden-tanned forty-year-old with the insane eyes of all this type – I remind you that next to the schoolteachers these female hyenas are among the most rabid of our Hitlerite whirling dervishes.

And what reaction was there? Did these Bavarian farmers, offspring of independent-minded fathers prepared at any time to revolt – did they at least dip the lady, all on fire as she was with a burning readiness to die, into Lake Obing?

The thought never entered their minds. They trailed off towards home, shaking their heads bewilderedly, muttering to each other that unfortunately there was nothing to be done.

On the other hand, there are the workers in a Munich electrical plant who are said to have electric irons ready for the great day of reckoning when the swastika is branded into Nazi foreheads. A fine idea, which needs only the addition of a single detail to be quite perfect: how would it be if they were forced to wear brown shirts for the rest of their lives?

9 October 1944

Herr Giesler has dreamed up a new surveillance technique. 'Housing Commissions' have now made their appearance in every town and village, empowered to enter and search any house at any hour of the day or night, to commandeer living space. Since they also have been put in charge of 'Labour Allocation' they can, at their own sweet will, force any woman whom they decide is not 'committed' to perform 'voluntary labour'.

This is what happened at our house: Like a bolt from the blue, without prior announcement of any kind, without knocking or ringing the bell, there appeared in the living-room the little dictator who was assigned to our quiet village a week ago, and who has spent the time since in a fruitless attempt to root out 'God be praised!'[63] as a greeting form among the farmers. Along with two other rooms, he took over my library, accompanying this with the amiable promise that a woman with at least three children would be quartered in each room, and to accommodate the horde, holes would be drilled in the Gothic walls and floors. I was ordered to move my library (including irreplaceable first editions, prints, and hand-copied manuscripts) down to the cellar where they could be quietly devoured by the mice. 'Don't get worked up, there are lots of book collections going down the drain. Why not yours?'

His eyes as he said this glistened with meanness: the one-time tax clerk was swollen to the size of a Napoleon in the consciousness of his own power. I can remember that during the First World War, the occupants of a dug-out fed their stove with first editions and priceless manuscripts from the castle of Mesothen at Liévin. But this was a simple case of soldiers in need, a simple reaching out after the first thing available, there was no spiteful feeling in it....

But what was happening here was something else. To begin with, in the case of this subordinate bureaucrat, there was the resentment of the educated man, the resentment of everything that was more than he was – and the feeling that now, finally, his chance had come, the long-awaited chance to revenge himself on a higher-caste man.

But there was something else involved: the canaille's hatred for all that is of the spirit. It was this hatred which allowed the German bourgeoisie in the middle of the nineteenth century to throw away everything that was best from their own past, an act unprecedented in its cynicism....

There was much to be done in the days that followed. At Traunstein, an Army officer had warned me: Herr Buchner had me on his list for my 'God-be-praised' greeting. This, plus his statement, widely reported, that I had been involved in the attempted assassination on 20 July, made it imperative that I at once find 'bombed-out' people who shared my ideas, who would not try to spy out the radio stations we listened to, and who were not denouncers. We took in a couple, upholsterers from Munich, whom I knew to be dependable, and then a 'bombed-out' artist was recommended to me, an American who had thus far gone on living undisturbed in Munich, and who, incidentally, turned out to be a tremendously good fellow. All this took a vast amount of time, since a man is on no account supposed to be able to choose who is to stay in his house, and therefore there were endless trips to Munich, in filthy, overcrowded trains, and interminable waits in the ante-rooms of Nazi functionaries, having to listen to the giggles of the well-tended females in all the surrounding offices – repellent types, whose distinguishing features are the permanent hair-do falling over the shoulder, the never-ending consumption of questionable ice-cream and still more questionable biscuits, and the tyrannising of the public.

Thus, while immense convulsions shake Nazidom at every point, I am enmeshed in a life in which there are times when I do not know whether my house still belongs to me or not. And yet, paradoxically, I am also getting deep insights into this whole tottering structure as I go about it.

My pilgrimage took me to the headquarters of the so-called Gauleiter, which is just exactly what one imagines a Nazi office to be like, complete with 'executive officers' who were office managers before they began impersonating Genghis Khan – and a smell in the air of secret fear, concealed behind a façade of coarseness and brutality, or else transformed into a reaching after sympathy.

On the other hand, there is the Gestapo, which I entered with the help of an appropriate letter, and which looks very different from what one imagines: quiet, dignified offices, courteous subordinates, and a responsible officer, a Councillor Gade, a polite and tactful young man who asked leave to finish his cigar, and was, generally, the very model of a man of breeding and poise. The Gestapo's greeting is 'God be praised!' while at the district office one is almost deafened with the bellowed 'Heil Hitler'.

When I described the perspective posed for me by the Gauleiter's underling of having to live under the threat of having my house searched at any time, the Gestapo official actually indicated that the element of force standing behind such threat – which could only mean the Nazi Party – must certainly come to an end in fourteen days or three weeks.

Strange atmosphere, compounded of fear, of resignation, and of a last, bellowing madness, which is to culminate now in Germany's turning itself into a heap of rubble in honour of the great Manitou – strange atmosphere, diseased with the microbes of the end of the world!

Imagine, however, that these termites, morning and evening

clinging to the trams like grapes – imagine that they go on: head-less as they have been made by the destruction of the intelligentsia, that they go on functioning! The air is so charged with tension that tomorrow, at any moment, lightning may flash. Except for those hardy souls who continue to down their daily portion of Nazi opti-mism, people know this, and are deeply resentful; their resentment emerges in the disputes which are constantly taking place, at post office windows, on trams, on these stupid queues waiting to procure what now goes under the name of newspapers.

Nerves are rubbed raw, and at any moment an argument may break out, followed by hand-to-hand grappling. I saw a sixteen-year-old female waiting to get on a tram slap a rather helpless old man because he was getting out too slowly. The sweet young thing was extremely astonished when I returned the compliment to her two-fold – in the face, incidentally, to the protesting murmurs of the canaille.

I never before saw such things here. The way people dealt with each other under the Munich Revolutionary Republic was a model of politeness compared to what there will be after Hitler. Munich, defiled and distorted as it is, devastated like all the other cities, by the Prussian locusts, has a strange look to me now, as though, walking in it, I were in Chicago.

Oh, it is dreadful to wander among the ruins of a city which only yesterday was like a good-humoured mother. As I rode down one street, a house collapsed in an immense cloud of dust, covering the trolley tracks we had just passed with a pile of rubble five metres high. As I write, I can smell the stench of decaying bodies, because under the ruins are the corpses of seventeen bank employees who were buried by the rubble. In pious commemora-tion, and to mark the place where these poor devils were drowned when a river of human excreta suddenly flooded out at them from the broken sewers, the survivors have placed a cross on top of the rubble heap, and the rats, grown plump with much gorging on corpses, rustle undisturbed over ruins and cross.

There are no telephone lines still in working order, and there is no service window without its lines of people waiting for hours alongside; nor is there a store with anything for sale, or a roof into which the rain does not come. And through it all, this herd of troglodytes goes on, brainless and animal, morning and evening charging into the restaurants after ration-free food like the apes at the zoo after they have been kept waiting for the noon feeding. They gulp down their chemical beer, believe every bit of propaganda larded out to them, and are basically responsible for the fact that twelve years could pass during which we have been ruled by a maniac. Is it not the absolute height of tragedy, simply inconceivable shame, that just those Germans who are left of the best of them, who have been prisoners of this herd of evil-tempered apes for twelve years, should wish and pray for the defeat of their own country, for the sake of that same country?

October 1944

Arrests, and more arrests. There is getting to be something akin to an arrest psychosis, which barely serves to conceal the terrible fear of the arresters.

Toni Arco[64] has been arrested. I am sure he bitterly regrets his assassination twenty-five years ago of Eisner. Schacht[65] has been arrested, and old Hugenberg.[66] Mayor Scharnagl[67] has been arrested, and old ladies connected with royalty, and young religious novices.

People disappear without trace. Nothing is heard of them for weeks and months. Whole families are separated in this way and sent off into the night. A. has been arrested; F.R. is also said to be in prison, his brother who holds the title of count disappeared without trace in the course of a trip to Vienna. All that is known of him is that he was seen in handcuffs between two guards on a station platform somewhere in Austria. Barely two years ago, both of his sons were swallowed up in this war.

Strange and grim news has been received about His Majesty.[68] Herr v. M. has received the following word from northern Italy: 'Do not worry about the Colonel, he is safe in the Dolomites.' In the context, there is no question that by the 'Colonel' is meant the 75-year-old King of Bavaria – the monarch who dipped into the store of memories of his youth to tell me such absorbing stories about his meeting with old Emperor Franz Joseph, and with Bismarck, and who described so well the enviable appetite of ninety-year-old Wilhelm I at the breakfast table, and who now evidently is forced to wander from one mountain retreat to the other in a foreign land.

Herr v. M. received this letter at the beginning of October. Now, at the end of the month, rumour has it that the King has been killed. The Nazis could hardly sink lower. I, however, can conceive of situations in which an enemy struck dead may be more dangerous than one left alive.

And on the thirteenth, a beautiful, burning-hot day in October, I was myself arrested.

At six in the morning – that hour so beloved of all secret police officials – I heard the bell ringing rather loudly, and saw below our Seebruck gendarme, a good soul, who explained apologetically that he had come in performance of what was for him the unpleasant assignment of conveying me to the Army jail at Traunstein.

I confess that I was not greatly concerned. Four days before, I had ignored a so-called 'call to arms' for service with the Volkssturm, citing an attack of *angina pectoris*. Immediately thereafter, however, I had gone like any good citizen to regional headquarters to explain, and the opinion there had been that a man who had only just received word that his son was missing in Russia might well be believed regarding illness.

I made a mistake. Deception, the burning-hot autumn day with its gay colours; deception, the tact, bordering almost on shame, of the gendarme. We crossed the river on our way to the train, and the melancholy with which my womenfolk waved to me from the house made me thoughtful. A couple of hours later I knew that this was, indeed, more than a little warning.

The gate of the Army post closed heavily behind me. Between me and the bright autumn day there was a fence and a highly martial guard. I was standing in a guard post filled with the smell of leather, sweat, and lard, the chief personage of which was a young Swabian sergeant – a man with that peculiarly Germanic combination of choler, activity, and exactitude which never rings quite true, and which has caused so much evil in the world.

I telephoned the major who was officer-in-charge. A voice so frigidly vindictive that the quality of it emerged quite clearly out of the receiver told me that I was not there to ask questions, but to wait. Then I happened to see a young officer I knew bicycling across the compound. I called to him, but when he came refrained from taking his hand because, as I explained, I had been arrested and so, in the jargon of the old Kaiser's Army on the Eastern Front, I was 'lousy'. He laughed, gave me his hand, and himself telephoned. As the crackle sounded from the receiver, he grew pale. He hung up, and then informed me, several degrees more formally now, that I was charged with 'undermining the morale of the Armed Forces'. He bowed and left.

The penalty for 'undermining the morale of the Armed Forces' is the guillotine – the guillotine, on which the condemned man, as I heard recently, is granted the single act of grace of being blinded by a thousand-candlepower light just before the blade whistles downward, with the aftermath being one of the Lysol bottles of an anatomy class.

In the meantime, however, evening had come on. The guard post was now a dark box. I was locked up.

The cell is two paces wide and six feet long, a concrete coffin equipped with a wooden pallet, a dirty, evil-smelling spittoon, and a barred window high up on the wall. By climbing onto the pallet I can see a minuscule piece of the sky, the barracks compound, a section of the officer quarters, and behind, a pine forest: a pine forest of our lovely Bavarian plateau, which has nothing in common with this frenzy of Prussian militarism, this pestilence which has devastated Bavaria.

So much for the window. On the walls, the inevitable obsceni-ties and calculations of time still to be served – in weeks, days, hours, and minutes, even. Then, a veritable flood of Soviet stars, which gave the idea that the entire Red Army had been imprisoned here. And lastly, scratched into the concrete with a key, perhaps, the words, so very applicable to me: 'My God, why hast Thou forsaken me?' I read this, and darkness envelops me. This was written by a man as close to death as I am.

It is true that not one word has been said to confirm this idea. And yet, I cannot help registering the fact of this venomous animosity, which is intent on finding something against me, and would make of an ignored draft notice a matter for the hangman.

It might well be believed of a sixty-year-old man who had lived his life honourably and had just received word that his son was a prisoner of the Russians that a heart attack did not necessarily signify an 'undermining of the morale of the Armed Forces'. And this would hold true even if there were not extant a statement to this effect by the senior physician in the town of Prien.

But what is happening to me now has nothing to do with a draft notice.

A night spent in heavy, laboured breathing, while outside sounded the brutal Army noises. We who are buried alive here are not to be granted even the solace of a quiet night. When a door is closed it is slammed shut with full force. When a man asks to be led to the stinking hole called the toilet, there resounds down the corridor the filthy curses of the roused guard. At three in the morning, the relief stamps with elephant-tread on the parapet, and at five-thirty, despite the fact that our being up cannot possibly be of benefit to anyone, and that our being asleep cannot harm anyone, the doors are ripped open to the bellow of 'Up!' – just when one might be able to doze off after the worried, sleepless night.

I pondered the question of who was responsible for this, who it was whose amiable purpose it had been to deliver me up to the hangman. I thought about the District Leader whom I had taken to court for calling me a coward over my use of a watch-dog – and I reflected that he might have chosen this way of revenging himself on me for having lost the case. I thought about the senile old coffee-house orator whose mouthings of propaganda I had refused to applaud. And I thought about the housing commissar who found high treason in my customary greeting of 'God be praised', and whom I was twice obliged to throw out of my house despite the fact that he was 'on official business of the Governor'. I thought of all these small, crawling things now finding their nourishment in denunciation and the decay of our country – murderers, large- and small-scale, now operating under cover of 'full legality', who have no idea that tomorrow they may be the ones for whom the hangman reaches.

But I cannot enjoy the thought of what lies in store for them, and this fact makes me thoughtful. Strange: I have progressed. Ten years ago, I worked out plans for a terrible revenge upon them. And today? Today, I know that no such thing as 'revenge' exists, and that those passages in the Bible which emphasise this fact reflect an ancient, honourable wisdom. Revenge? Years ago, I took an old friend who had fallen into desperate straits into my house. He repaid my hospitality and my financial help by undermining my marriage. I beat him as hard as it is possible for one man to beat another. For three days afterwards, I experienced a feeling of relief.

And then? And then came the realisation that all of this would not weigh greatly in the scales of eternity. If I had ventured deeper into the things that are God's and had actually killed him, I would thereby have helped him to a heroic death, instead of the prolonging of a dishonourable life. I myself have been responsible for the tears of many; and has it ever failed that I have not paid for these tears, even if retribution was years in coming? Don't I know that the things that are happening to me now, the approach of death, the separation from my loved ones, the filth, the attempt to degrade me – that all these things will be required, even if I am not there to see to it?

A man need not be a Christian to know all this. But one must be a Christian to give form to this, and then heroically to live and die. In 1912, aboard an English coastal steamer, as untroubled a young man as only an innocent son of Wilhelmism could be, I theorised to the only other passenger, an old Chinese intellectual, in the course of an evening promenade on deck, that the whole of Christianity, everywhere in the world, now found itself in a single vast agony. The venerable old man, a follower of the precepts of Lao-tzu, professor of Asiatic religions at Tsingtao Academy, looked at me with amusement. Then he said quietly that Christianity still had before it its great and decisive task. I was deeply impressed by the way he spoke.

Today, thirty years later, bowed as I am under the weight of responsibility for certain major sins, having attained to a certain height on some few occasions and fallen to certain depths on others, I know the thing is not so simple. Certainly, Christianity still has its great work before it. But in the face of the Satanism which now prevails, a second Catacombs will be necessary and a second Nero's burning of Rome before the spirit may emerge victorious a second time.

14 October 1944

All that was entailed, supposedly, was a single night at a hotel, and so I had come with just a small valise. They searched it for weapons: It was not a good beginning. And when I asked for a lawyer, the response was harsh.

Soon I was in a cell, and standing (against regulations) on the plank bed could see out into the perfect autumn day. The right to be out in that perfection had been taken from me, stolen as surely as they have stolen from us those years that were the First World War, and those of the years of inflation of the Twenties, and the Hitler-years – a quarter of a century, the best of a man's life – robbed by these militarist maniacs.

Across the caserne yard in the officers' quarters, moving from room to room behind the cheap curtains considered elegant these days was a blond of the new officer breed, very likely yesterday a lavatory attendant into whose hand (the same hand which had just been clearing away various blockages and encumbrances) you slipped two marks. They have come up, these people, as far as we have gone down these last twelve years; obviously, since it is our money which has raised them up. The little schizophrenic who is their leader had nothing and was nothing, but from 1918 those like him in their rage began to puff him up into what he has become. What an Augean stable that will be, the one they leave for us to clean up!

Now they're marching on the parade-ground. I hear this from morning to night, the latest in military marches, *snappy* little melodies bellowed by a leader sheep, shouted back by his flock of 250. Shattering, these idiotic songs, these faces, this spiritual castration-by-propaganda. They march and rumble past – here, five men attached to one machine, there, a lumbering behemoth belching clouds of stinking gas with ten aboard, then another new mechanical monster with another five. What do these iron-plated apparitions have to do with soldiers? Better take the regimental insignia off their uniforms, and sew on instead gold-threaded representations of screwdrivers, or oil cans!

I want to be clear: I come from a long line of soldiers. At seventeen, on a horse behind the silver kettle-drums, that is exactly what I felt myself to be – a soldier. But the coming of the machine gun and the four-cylinder engine has raised a question, and that is, does the profession of soldier still exist, any more than that of statesman, or king, or poet or intellectual – supplanted as these have been by surrogates – so that all that's left among the traditional professions is that of licensed whore. (And even the public whore is close to being regulated out of existence, with the woman being required twice each session, at foreplay and at climax, to shout a politically knowledgeable 'Heil Hitler!') As for me, I can see myself ending as a pacifist ... not because I set that much store by the inherently fragile artifacts of this world; no, because I want to officiate at the funeral of a damnable lie – the lie that the concept of 'soldier' can be infinitely further perverted!

This afternoon, I was brought to a hearing. This was done before a captain wearing the insignia of a former noncom,[69] and the look of a decent Bavarian *petit bourgeois* (he could have been a clerk behind a post-office counter, or in a busy law office). Still, when I declared that what had brought me here was foul denunciation, the machinations of a low intriguer, these attractive features contorted and he blared at me like a tuba. I waited until all this lung power was exhausted, and then, looking him earnestly in the eyes, ventured that at the moment a defenceless man stood there before him – with emphasis on *at the moment*.

Then there flooded down on my head a veritable torrent of accusation:

– I had falsely stated my rank (to which I responded that in the course of my life I had waded in too much blood to give undue importance to rank).

– That in the course of my earlier admission of wrongdoing, I had made light of the People's Militia. With my statement before me, I proceeded to show that the very opposite was the case.

– That I had organised a demonstration of women protesting against the removal of crucifixes from public buildings, did not say 'Heil Hitler' when I should have, and downplayed the value of the German currency.

I answered with a question: was I being questioned here under military or Party auspices? Also, in the matter of the currency charge, could I get further details?

This was not a fruitful approach. What followed was a torrent of invective that burst over me like burning lava, covering all argument, all protest. I was silent. They took me away.

But I was not to get off so lightly. They called in the major, and when I saw him I knew: only a Higher Power could save me now. He was an apparition, a man-doll, a frightful stumbling puppet smashed by shot and shell and put together with prostheses. Nothing worked naturally, nothing was normal – the man was a mechanical horror. And in the eyes, that sadism....

I know the type. I saw them in the time of the Free Corps.[70] These unholy apparitions, filled with sadistic rage, moved through that time as they do today, officers now under the Nazi regime, mutilated beings involved in inconceivable crime.

Again now I am alone. Far away, over that house and land I call home, there would be the last red flash of sunset; inside here, the clumping of boots as the food detail goes by. Strange how quickly a man is brought down to the lowest levels of preoccupation in prison through trying any trick to make life here easier. You learn to clean the malodorous corners of the cell without disgust, and to lie down on the insect-infested straw mattress without a qualm. Your suit, measured by a London tailor whose greeting on the occasional shopping trip could have been directed to a reigning prince, is rubbed to threads on the splintery plank-bed, and you hardly care....

And what a thing it is that these little tricks, while they do indeed make your life easier, swiftly bring you down to jailhouse level. Some well-meaning bloke slides back the lock on your door, and freedom suddenly is the equivalent of being out of your cell, walking up and down alongside the door. You don't actually do it; the thought has to suffice.

The following day, now further enmeshed in this society of the imprisoned, I myself slide back the bolts and thus for the first time get to see, face to face, this brotherhood of the damned, my neighbours in the concrete cells. Until now they have been known only by their signals, the tapping on the walls in the code I quickly learned. Beyond the flat, blank sales-clerk visages, beyond the dead-white, stupid faces of the little underlings and clerks dropped into Army uniforms as guards is this polyglot Commune of prisoners. Among these, Poles, Czechs (even Danes and Norwegians) tumbled into this place like dice from a cup, are those who provide the balm of real people – as though, in a foreign country, one were to hear for the first time the sound of one's own language:

– A tearful little fellow, rather insufficiently attired in a shirt of the Moroccan Guards, but as hairy and lumbering as a bear, in deep depression. He had overstayed his leave by five days, seduced by a local maiden and the carp-fishing and -eating pleasures her family's pond afforded.

– L., an honest, dinaric[71] horseface, unfortunately a more serious case. Filled with hatred against these latter-day Communards, he wandered in civilian limbo for five months, and then was picked up at a military checkpoint, where he was also found, unfortunately, to be carrying a loaded revolver – yes, a very

grave matter. The soldier who arrested him, tool of this proletarian militarism that he is, actually whispered to him in an access
of humanity that he now regretted having done so. Indeed, the
case is serious; it could even cost him his head.

– T., Croat, is accused of having had dealings with the Russians
somewhere on the periphery of the empire – a bonehead drafted
and flung at random into an Army unit with which he has as much
connection as I do with a man from Mars – actually, a young
fellow of quality, friendly, likeable, even somewhat cultivated by
the standards of this pesthole. In the dark corner of the cell, alongside an infested straw mattress, we talked for a time about his
distant homeland. He described how the Serbs evacuated his
peaceful winegrowers' village by the Danube because they wanted
to settle their own people there.

'Believe me, the harvest was good; the barns were filled with
wheat, the vats full of rye, the shed floors covered with sheaves of
maize and tobacco. That spring, actually, there had been rumours
that we were going to be forced off our land, and these rumours
were believed by our gloomy old folks. But we who were the youth
laughed at these fears, and were confirmed in our confidence by
the Serbian officials, who vehemently denied any such plans....
Yes, just two days before it all became reality, they announced strict
penalties for spreading rumours of the kind.

'So you can imagine what a shock it was when it actually
happened. We were given just twelve days to leave our village, our
vineyards, the rich harvest in our sheds. We were told that in
exchange for leaving behind all our goods, all our property, all our
farm machinery, we would find the equivalent in Bosnia, with
completely equipped farmsteads and rich crops ... in short, that we
would not regret the change.

'The old people knew what the truth was. That same night
many cut their throats, others hanged themselves, or drowned
themselves in the Danube. As for the rest of us, we let them dump
us into a miserable typhus-ridden collection point. Then we were

shipped in sealed freight cars, and for fourteen days lived and died in the stench of our own faeces and the discharges of the dead.

'Once arrived, part of us were locked into the freezing cold room of a large estate; others were thrown into the half-destroyed greenhouses of an abandoned nursery; while a third group was put into barracks filled with lice, formerly used for people ill with typhus. These, sir, were the "equally prosperous" farms we had been promised!'

'The old regime,' I answered, 'the Austro-Hungarian Empire, would not have been less cruel. Do you imagine that all it required of you was to pledge allegiance to the double eagle, the symbol of the imperial throne in Vienna?'

'Granted, sir, and still one wants to lead one's own life.'

He meant by this one's own nationalist life, the insanity which has spread from 1789 on, in whose flames Europe will be consumed – and which could only burn so destructively because the milder flame of a generalised European intellectuality, the flame of those who seek God on this earth, has been extinguished.

I lay down sadly. I have been born too early on this planet. I will not survive this insanity.

... Sad days, of wind coming through the cracks in the walls, of the disappearance of the faint autumn sun, of the coming, so quickly, of the apocalyptic hour of dusk in this stone coffin.

While the light lasts, until the day dies, I go on reading, despairingly, these utterly stupid memoirs, these diaries suffused with a special Parisian arrogance, these orgiastic survivals of the rotting-away of the Napoleonic concept, whose death-throes have for so long poisoned our lives....

'Formerly, there was a wide area of differentiation – now, there is total equality. Formerly also, there was something called fate – now, it is the daily wage. Renown – what is that? Weigh out a kilo of renown for me – how much? We buy bridges for our mouths, cultivate intestinal flora in our stomachs. We parcel out pieces of life among each other, leave each other less and less of the air, from generation to generation leave behind an increasingly mishandled and chaotic world. The princess? She rides a bicycle the way the workers under her father, the king, did, and they barely move aside when she comes by, and may or may not greet her.'

So, in 1915, wrote the man who, shortly afterward, driven of course by the women of his family with their need to bulk large in the world, joined the camp of these same mass-men.[72]

On one of the first cold days of the year, I was called to a hearing, and was astounded at the changes which had occurred behind the scenes. Where just a couple of days earlier there had been icy northern winds, now a warm breeze caressed me; where only yesterday this crude, bellowing captain yelled at me like a top sergeant, now he dealt with me with the utmost consideration, and I was almost fearful that he would end this evening hearing by releasing me with a good-night kiss.

The mystery was soon resolved. Out of the office of the major in charge, clad in a fantastic black leather overcoat bearing the emblem of the SS, came General Dtl., and it is to him that I owe the bringing-about of this miracle. A decade younger than me, he chided me gently, a discourse which of course I did not know whether I was to take seriously, or whether it was meant to ring well in his own ears. In any case, the effect on the corporal-turned-captain was noteworthy.

'Does the Herr General require a car, or does he intend to go by foot?' said in true Prussian barracks jargon, and with a passion that gave one to think that in the next moment this booted lackey would either fall on his face before him or simply jump up and disappear into thin air.

And so occurred the miracle which I, just an hour earlier, entombed in my cell, had not dared to conceive: I was to be released that very night.

I was led out, had myself locked back in, and experienced what probably every prisoner about to be released goes through: hours of uncertainty in which the fear is that at the very last minute something will happen. You look, ridiculously, for a sign, anything to relieve the tension: the end-time, which is almost as bad as the first hours in the shock of jail.

Luckily for me, an air-raid shortened the time: gawked at like animals from the zoo by assorted typists, laundresses and kitchen help, we were taken down to a narrow, low-ceilinged cellar where pipes connected with all the various water- and toilet-outlets. Presumably, we would be better off drowning in excrement-filled sewage than being split apart by shrapnel fragments in the open air....

Through the cellar window I could make out a small piece of sky and a somewhat larger section of the caserne courtyard. Ah, unrelieved monotony of these endless windows, bareness of sheds, apocalyptic ugliness in every direction – a hideousness which seems to be the very essence of militarism.... They hate everything which might carry a hint of spirituality and beauty. What they worship is a fetish, probably something like a grotesquely enlarged *dice-cup*. And out of this affinity for the ugly they have constructed a religion at whose shrine all the world is to worship.

No, they will be rooted out, they will be pursued remorselessly, reduced to their true level by every conceivable and inconceivable means that can be found to humiliate them, because only then, when all memory of them has been blotted-out, will there be peace in the world.

Two hours later, leaving the caserne, I had the feeling of a man buried in a mass grave – filthied, filled with unmanning memories.

An ancient superstition forbids it that the person who has emerged into freedom look back, lest he be returned. Indeed I kept on going, never looking back, but then my friend the corporal came running up with a brush and cleaned off my dusty coat, saying: 'Make this thing end *soon!*'

For you, my young friend: in the name of our shared hatred: in the name of tormented mankind: in the name of the world....

Once at home, I learned what was thought to be happening to me, and what indeed would have happened had it not been for the intervention of Dtl.

Notes

1. August Albers was found on the tracks near Tutzing, on Lake Starnberg. The assumption is that he had decided to commit suicide following the death of Spengler.

2. At that time, Oswald Spengler lived at 54 Agnesstrasse, Munich.

3. Founded in 1871, the Langnamverein was a kind of National Association of Manufacturers in western Germany. The industrialists of the Ruhr were especially influential in it.

4. An error: Spengler's work was on Heraclitus.

5. The widely circulated rumour that the second volume of Oswald Spengler's *The Hour of Decision* was safe in a Swiss bank vault, in manuscript, later proved to be false. As H. Kornhardt notes, in his foreword to the new edition of Spengler's work, issued in 1953, 'Part Two was never written.'

6. Hermann Esser, an old-time Nazi, was named Bavarian Minister Without Portfolio and head of the Chancellery in 1933, Bavarian Minister of Economics in 1934, and President of the Reich's Office of Foreign Travel in 1936.

7. The vastly complex series of circumstances leading up to the so-called Assumption of Power by Hitler in 1933, and his being named Chancellor, is described by, among others, Alan Bullock, in his *Hitler: A Study in Tyranny*. About the Eastern Relief Scandal, Bullock writes that a conversation between Hitler and Oskar von Hindenburg on the subject took place on 22 January 1933, in the course of which Hitler 'threatened' that 'he would launch an investigation of the Eastern Relief Scandal that could lead to damaging revelations about German President Paul von Hindenburg, and the exposure of the role Oskar von Hindenburg had played in it, as well as illegal use of public funds for the Hindenburgs' Neudeck estate.' There is no reference to Oskar von Hindenburg's '13-million mark bank loan outstanding' in Bullock's book (New York: Harper & Row, Publishers, revised edition, 1964). Nor does any mention of this appear in *Die Auflösung der Weimarer Republik* by Karl D. Bracher

(Villinger/Schwarzwald, 1964), or in *Die Junker und die Weimarer Republik: Charakter und Bedeutung der Osthilfe in den Jahren 1928–33*, by Bruno Buchta (East Berlin, 1959).

8. 'Bohemian' here is a geographic reference.

9. The Potempa murder refers to the killing of Communist worker Konrad Pietrzuch in his home in the Silesian village of Potempa by a number of SA men on 9 August 1932. The men involved were tried and convicted of the murder. Hitler's telegram following the trial read: 'My comrades! In the face of this unrelentingly vengeful verdict, I feel eternally bound to you. As of this moment, your freedom has become a matter of the honour of all of us, and the battle against a regime under which such things are possible, our duty. Adolf Hitler.' The storm troopers were later amnestied.

10. The strike against the Berlin Transport Authority was begun by the Communists, joined by the Nazis, and lasted from 3–7 November 1932.

11. In the days before the Nazis came to power, Gregor Strasser was the Party's organisational secretary. However, in the course of inner-party battles, he opposed first Goebbels and then Hitler. He resigned his party posts in 1932. He was killed on 30 June 1934, in the course of the Röhm Putsch.

12. No Frau von Schröter can be located in the records of the time in this connection. Probably Reck-Malleczewen is referring to the conversation between Hitler and Franz von Papen early in January 1933, at the home of Kurt von Schröder, the Cologne banker. There were later conversations between the two at Ribbentrop's house in Berlin.

13. For more on the role of Kurt von Schleicher in all of this; and about the rumour of the arrest of Oskar von Hindenburg; as well as about the attempt to prevent Hitler from coming to power, in which Kurt von Bredow played a part, see German sources, including *Reichswehr, Staat und NSDAP*, by Thilo Vogelsang (Stuttgart, 1962), and the Bracher work previously cited.

14. One eye-witness to the deathbed scene between Hindenburg and Hitler on 1 August 1934, has described it this way: 'Hindenburg was at the point of death when Hitler entered the room. Besides the doctors, his two daughters were present. Apparently he did not recognise Hitler. In any case, he paid no attention to him. He had gone back in his mind to a time and people more understandable to him. The last words he uttered were: "My Kaiser ..." And then, impossible to say in what context he meant them: "My Fatherland" or "My German Fatherland ..." He could

be understood only with difficulty. Then he was silent. Hitler once admitted to an Army aide years later that Hindenburg's last words had been about the Kaiser, and not about himself.' (Translated from Walter Görlitz, *Hindenburg: Ein Lebensbild*, Bonn, 1953.)

15. General Max Hoffmann served with Ludendorff from 1914–16, then took command of German troops stationed on the Russian front and represented Germany at Brest Litovsk, when Russia agreed to get out of the war.

16. Willi Schmid was the music critic of the *Münchner Neuesten Nachrichten*. He was mistaken for another Willi Schmid and shot by the Nazis in the course of the Röhm Putsch.

17. In 1950 it was learned that Gustav Ritter von Kahr, who in 1923 headed the Bavarian government which put down Hitler's attempt on 23 November to seize power, was badly beaten in the course of being delivered to Dachau in June 1934, and then shot. His corpse reportedly was uncovered on the moor near the concentration camp.

18. In Bad Wiessee, in June 1934, Hitler ordered a number of arrests. He did not, however, either carry out any executions on the spot, or order them. He met no resistance at the time.

19. Clemens Freiherr von Franckenstein was a composer, and in 1914–18, and again from 1924–34, director of the Bavarian Court (later, State) Theatre.

20. Ernst Hanfstaengl's nickname 'Putzi' dated from childhood. He was Nazi foreign press chief. His own account, later, of his flight from Germany concords almost exactly with what Reck-Malleczewen relates. Only a few details differ: the fact, for example, that it was not his 'eighty-year-old mother' who was sent to England to fetch him back, but a Göring emissary, a General Bodenschatz. See Ernst Hanfstaengl: *Hitler, the Missing Years*, London, 1957.

21. It is no longer widely believed – in Germany, in any case – that a Nazi directly set the Reichstag ablaze. In a book published in 1962 about the fire, called *Der Reichstagsbrand: Legende und Wirklichkeit* (Baden: Rastatt), author Fritz Tobias states unequivocally that the Dutchman van der Lubbe was alone in actually starting the conflagration. Hanfstaengl's only connection with the event, by his statement of it, came when he saw the glare in the sky from his windows nearby, and called Hitler at Goebbels' house.

22. Federal German archives contain a manuscript entitled (in German) 'Arnold Rechberg and the Problem of Germany's Orientation to the West after World War I'.

23. The woman who sheltered Hitler following the failure of his 9 November 1923 attempt to seize power was not Hanfstaengl's sister, Erna, but his wife, Helene. Hitler was arrested at the Hanfstaengl house at Uffing, Bavaria, two days later. (See Hanfstaengl, *op. cit.*) A letter from Erna Hanfstaengl has this to say about the 'Patroness' reference: 'I could hardly have been Hitler's "Patroness" since I never, after 1923, either saw or spoke to him.'

24. Unity Mitford, cousin by marriage of Winston Churchill and sister-in-law of Oswald Mosley, the English Fascist leader, is described in other sources as having hoped for marriage with Hitler. Reportedly, her attempt at suicide occurred in Munich's English Garden in September 1939. She died of inflammation of the brain in 1948.

25. '*Dass mir hier keener uff den Ofen ruffkommt.*'

26. Theodor Häcker's journal was published as *Tag- und Nachtbücher. 1933–45*, Munich, 1947.

27. Fritz Thyssen, a top German industrialist, supported the Nazis 'to save Germany from Bolshevism'. He opposed Germany's launching of war in 1939, emigrated to Switzerland, and then went to France where he was arrested by the Germans following their occupation of France. The Nazis first put him into a mental institution at Babelstadt, then confined him successively in the Oranienburg, Buchenwald, and Dachau concentration camps. The ending of the war meant for him only a change of jailers: he was imprisoned by the Americans. Released finally, he went to Argentina, where he died in 1951. His book, *I Paid Hitler*, was published in New York and Toronto in 1941.

28. By 'Royal Master' Reck-Malleczewen means Crown Prince Rupprecht of Bavaria.

29. Hitler talked about the ban on duels and the Strunck affair later. See *Hitler's Table Conversations, Tischgespraeche im Fuehrerhauptquartier, 1941–42*, edited by Henry Picker (Bonn, 1961).

30. Adolf Ziegler, whom the Nazis awarded their Gold Medal, was named professor of art at the Munich Academy by the Nazis in 1933, and then president of the Reich's Chamber for the Arts.

31. Information on a 'Red Anchor' band of teenaged resistants who derived from the Haidhausen and Giesing sections of Munich is lacking.

32. Austrian Chancellor Kurt von Schuschnigg was arrested by the Germans following the Anschluss. He was kept first in the Hotel Metropol in Vienna under SS guard; then in the Gestapo's Wittelsbach Palace centre in Munich. Sachsenhausen, Flossenbürg and Dachau concentration camps followed. After the war, Schuschnigg taught in the US. See 'Requiem in Red, White and Red'/Austrian Requiem, by Karl Schuschnigg (London, 1947).

33. The reference to the 'Jew-hunt staged by Goebbels' is to the Night of Crystal, 9 November 1938, when Jewish stores were broken into (leaving broken glass littering the pavements, hence the reference), and synagogues all over Germany were set on fire. A German work on the officially sponsored pogrom is *Der 9. November 1938. Reichskristallnacht*, by Hermann Graml, Bonn, 1953.

34. Hans Albers, the personification of masculinity to several generations of German women, was an actor and screen star perhaps most familiar to the rest of the world for his part in *The Blue Angel* with Marlene Dietrich.

35. By 'D.' Reck-Malleczewen may be referring to the legal officer of the Bavarian Infantry Regiment in which Hitler served as courier in the First World War, a Dr Diess. A German work on this period of Hitler's life is *Der Mann, der Feldherr werden wollte*, by Fritz Wiedemann, (Velbert, 1964).

36. Hitler was awarded the Iron Cross, First Class in World War I. Wiedemann says he earned it.

37. In the course of the abortive coup of 1923, Hitler badly injured his left shoulder. As noted, above, he then fled to Uffing.

38. Hitler never lived on Barerstrasse in Munich, but the Nazi organ, the *Völkische Beobachter*, was published on that street.

39. In 1939, Göring visited Madrid, and while there wanted to confer the newly created German 'Special Order of the German Eagle' decoration on Spanish Chief of State Francisco Franco. Franco, however, had not forgotten that the year before, when he had offered a Spanish decoration to Hitler, the latter had refused it.

40. Bruno Brehm was awarded the German National Book Prize in 1939.

41. The Fount of Youth was the Nazi Lebensborn, an SS organisation under the direct supervision of SS Chief Heinrich Himmler, which was assigned the following functions:

(a) To provide support for large families of racially and biologically valuable antecedents.
(b) To provide facilities and care for racially and biologically valuable prospective mothers, under the assumption that these will bring similarly valuable offspring into the world.
(c) To care for such offspring.

(d) To care for the mothers of such offspring.

During the war, the Lebensborn, from a publication of which the above is taken, ran children's homes in which children from the occupied areas were placed and reared under new names as Germans. The use of SS men as 'studs' in the way Reck-Malleczewen describes was widely believed, but has, say German sources, no foundation in fact.

42. On 8 November 1939, a bomb intended for Hitler exploded in Munich's Bürgerbräukeller, killing eight and wounding sixty people. The Nazi *Völkische Beobachter* announced that the assassination attempt was the work of the British Intelligence Service and Otto Strasser, disaffected Nazi. It now appears that the attempt was solely the conception of one man, a Georg Elser.

43. Alexander Glaser practised law in Munich. He was shot in 1934.

44. Christian Weber, a veteran Nazi, held a number of Party posts as well as Munich administrative functions. On familiar terms with Hitler, he was one of the typically equivocal luminaries of Nazism.

45. The Führer's order referred to here has never been found. Probably this was a word-of-mouth directive never committed to paper.

46. From 1938, Fritz Fischer was director of the Bavarian State Operetta Theatre.

47. Adolf Wagner was Nazi Gauleiter of the Oberpfalz region and Greater Munich. Paul Giesler took over his functions following Wagner's death in 1944.

48. Friedrich Karl Freiherr von Eberstein headed the Munich police from 1936 to 1941.

49. Helmut Oldenbourg was chief of the Nazi Motor Corps for Bavaria. He died in 1957.

50. Julius Streicher published the anti-Semitic *Der Stürmer* and was Nazi Gauleiter of Franconia. In 1946, he was convicted of crimes against humanity by the International Military Tribunal in Nuremberg, and sentenced to death. Earlier, Streicher's Party posts had been taken away from him by Hitler, although he retained the title of Gauleiter, and his newspaper.

51. In 1931, Hitler's niece was found shot in his Munich apartment. It was assumed that she had committed suicide.

52. The invasion of Russia.

53. Count Friedrich von Schulenburg was German Ambassador to Russia from 1934–41.

54. A Reich Office for Ethics in Business never existed in the Nazi governmental apparatus.

55. In the interim between the time the Soviet Army left the Ukraine and the German Army marched in, some western Ukrainians in Lemberg organised a bloody pogrom of their own. A Nazi publication of the time hailed the 'praise-worthy moves against the Jews'.

56. The *Black Corps* was a weekly published by the SS. The editor was Gunter d'Alquen.

57. Ernst Niekisch was arrested by the Nazis in 1937. In 1939, he was sentenced to life in prison. He was freed at the end of the war. The newspaper he published (until 1934) was called *Widerstand* (Resistance).

58. Gerhard Rossbach was a well-known leader of the right-wing semi-official army called the Free Corps after World War I.

59. There is no mention of a Fuchs in the available literature on the Scholl case. Roland Freisler was the president of the People's Court before which the two young people were tried and sentenced to death, and Freisler also was responsible for the convictions of those involved in the attempted coup of 20 July 1944.

60. Christoph Probst's mother took the name of Kleeblatt following her second marriage. Young Probst, a medical student, was hanged with the Scholls in 1943.

61. The pun is evident only in the original, which depends upon a play on the word *lügt* (meaning 'lies', in the sense of untruths).

62. Maria Olczewska was a famous German opera star.

63. '*Grüss Gott!*' (God be praised!) is the old and standard way of greeting in southern Germany and Austria.

64. Count Anton 'Toni' von Arco auf Valley shot Bavarian Minister-President Kurt Eisner in 1919. He was imprisoned for a short time in 1933, and then again in 1944, following the 20 July attempt. He died in 1945.

65. Hjalmar Schacht was president of the Reichsbank and from 1934–37 Minister of Economics in the Nazi regime. He was sent to the Flossenbürg concentration camp in 1944, and was later found innocent of charges preferred against him before the International Military Tribunal.

66. Alfred Hugenberg, who was chairman of the German National People's Party, and for half of 1933 Minister of the Economy, was not arrested in the period of the Third Reich.

67. Karl Scharnagl resigned as mayor of Munich in 1933. He was

imprisoned in Dachau for a time in 1944. From 1945–49 he was again Munich's mayor. He died in 1963.

68. Crown Prince Rupprecht of Bavaria never relinquished his rights to the throne, and was, as a result, considered to be the 'King of Bavaria' by many people. He was extremely popular with Bavarians. He died in 1955.

69. The reference is to the 100,000-man *Reichswehr* allowed to Germany under the Treaty of Versailles. Noncoms in that army were often made officers when the German army was vastly expanded, in defiance of the Treaty, under the Nazi regime.

70. Free Corps (*Freikorps*): Paramilitary units which ranged over Germany after World War I, generally used to put down leftwing revolts and uprisings.

71. 'dinaric', *Oxford English Dictionary*, 2nd ed.: 'A racial type, indicating people inhabiting the coast of the northern Adriatic, characterised by tall stature, a very short head, dark wavy hair and straight or aquiline nose'.

72. The source of this quote is obscure. Reck does not elaborate.